# Husband Killer Kristy Fulgham An Anthology of True Crime

Jessi Dole

Published by Trellis Publishing, 2021.

While every precaution has been taken in the preparation of this book, the publisher assumes no responsibility for errors or omissions, or for damages resulting from the use of the information contained herein.

HUSBAND KILLER KRISTY FULGHAM AN ANTHOLOGY OF TRUE CRIME

**First edition. June 29, 2021.**



ISBN: 979-8224563371

Written by Jessi Dole.

# HUSBAND KILLER KRISTY FULGHAM

## JESSI DOLE

It was no secret that Joey and Kristi Fulgham were dealing with some pretty serious marital problems. The couple had even appeared on an episode of "The Montel Williams Show," to address Kristi's many infidelities. The mother of three was facing her own issues, and was looking for a way to get out of the failing marriage.

**"They were addicted to each other."**

Born in 1976, Kristi had grown up in Starkville, Mississippi – home of Mississippi State University, but that was about it. She was still very young when her parents divorced, and she lived with her mother. According to those who knew her, Kristi managed to grow into a happy, easy-going child – despite the turmoil that surrounded her.

"She kept everyone happy and smiling and laughing," said Tyler Edmonds, Kristi's half-brother. "It was just, kind of, really hard to not like Kristi."

But as Kristi became a teenager, it wasn't her laugh or her easy-going nature that attracted men to her. Her infectious smile was second only to her good looks.

"She was obviously a gorgeous girl, just extremely attractive," said Jim Waide, who represented Tyler Edmonds in court. "Men, apparently, just fell all over her."

She seemed to enjoy the attention, too – in high school, she dated a wide selection of different men. According to Jim Waide, she would "just go from one to the next." Her life seemed to revolve around the various men she was seeing, and she appeared to be in no hurry to settle down.

But in 1991, Kristi married Joey Fulgham. Initially, they seemed to have a lot in common.

"Joey was kind of our class clown," recalled Tommy Whitfield, an investigator with the Oktibbeha County's Sheriff's Department who went to high school with Joey. "He always joked around, was always in a good mood, always made everybody happy."

According to Tyler Edmonds, Joey was "a blue-collar" guy who loved tinkering with old cars. He'd also served in the National Guard, and was very patriotic. But when he met Kristi, she seemed to take priority over everything else.

"They were addicted to each other," Tyler said. "They could never seem to leave each other alone."

Together, they raised three children – and had taken on the responsibility of helping care for Kristi's much younger half-brother, Tyler. The two shared a biological father, and had reconnected after years apart. Kristi had been 13 when Tyler was born, and since they each lived with their individual mothers, they hadn't spent much time together. But when Tyler was 11, his mother was struggling to make ends meet, and Kristi decided to help out – she spent time with Tyler after school and on weekends.

"I think my sister wanted that relationship," explained Tyler. "She would come pick me up and take me to her house for the weekend, and we'd all hang out. I really clung to her – she was a very loving, caring sister."

"Tyler basically worshipped the ground Kristi walked upon," said Tommy Whitfield.

But as Kristi and Tyler's relationship grew closer, her marriage to Joey had started falling apart. According to Tyler, they argued about "anything and everything." She would even move out for months at a time, bouncing from house to house while they tried to work things out.

"There were rumours and speculation that she was continuing to see multiple men at the same time," said Ben Bounds, a former reporter with the Starkville Daily News who covered the case as it broke.

Kristi denied the rumours, when they made their way to her husband, Joey, but he became paranoid that she was cheating on him. When she gave birth to their youngest child, he even had a DNA test performed to ensure that the new baby was biologically his – but as it turned out, she wasn't.

Still, Joey was committed to his marriage and his family – and he confirmed this on national television, when Kristi took him on "The Montel Williams Show" in 2000.

"He said it didn't matter who she belonged to, that he was going to be her daddy and love her just like the other two," Kristi told Montel in the segment.

"I love her," Joey said. "I mean, I really do."

But in March of 2002, Kristi took the children and moved out of the family's Starkville home – and into a new house with Kyle Harvey, her boyfriend at the time. By May of 2003, they had returned to the home they shared with Joey, though, and the couple began attempting to repair the damage that Kristi's infidelity had done to their relationship.

**A holiday weekend gone wrong**

On May 11, Joey's body was found with a gunshot wound to the head. Kristi and her teenaged half-brother Tyler Edmonds had stopped at her place before heading up the Mississippi Gulf Coast for a quick weekend getaway to celebrate Mother's Day – and had shot Joey in the head, while he was fast asleep.

Kyle and Kristi met in 2002, and quickly began living together at his home in Jackson. According to Kyle's testimony, Kristi did move back to live with Joey, but had only planned to stay with him until she found a new home of her own. He said she would frequently return to Jackson, to check out real estate listings in an attempt to find a home for sale in the area. Kristi was unemployed at the time, Kyle said, but she intended to purchase the house with money she'd told Kyle that she would inherit from her grandmother - $300,000.

That Mother's Day weekend, May 9 to 11, 2003, Kyle and Kristi had arranged to take a trip up the coast to celebrate the holiday. According to Kyle, Kristi had offered to pay for the trip. After picking up her brother Tyler on the Friday night, she left Starkville with Tyler and the children at around 6:30 on Saturday morning – she called Kyle and told him they were on their way.

When Kyle came home from work that morning, between 10:30 and 11 a.m., he said Kristi, Tyler, and the three children were already waiting at his apartment. From there, he said, they headed up the coast – and he noticed that Kristi had a surprising amount of cash with her. She used the cash to buy food and souvenirs, and to pay for the room they stayed in at the Beau Rivage Hotel.

"For Mississippi, this is kind of like a little, mini-Vegas strip," Tyler explained. "There are casinos, restaurants, and beaches."

Saturday night was spent on the coast, Kyle testified, and the group arrived back in Jackson on Sunday evening, at around 5 p.m.

Meanwhile, Shannon Fulgham was starting to worry. He worked with his brother, Joey, at a local car dealership, where they received a paycheck each Friday at around noon. That Friday, on May 9, Joey had cashed a check for just more than $1,000, and had put the bills in his wallet. But Shannon hadn't seen him since they'd left work that day.

They had plans the next day to attend an air show together. Shannon called to meet up with Joey at around 11 a.m., but Joey hadn't answered the phone. When Shannon stopped by at around 12:15 p.m., he noticed that Joey's car was parked in the driveway, but Joey never came to the door. Furthermore, the door was locked, which was unusual.

"He had never had to knock on the door at his brother's house," said Ben Bounds. "He always walked right in the back door, because it was always unlocked – even when Joey wasn't home."

By late afternoon, Shannon still hadn't heard from his brother, so – sensing that something was wrong – he went back to the house and cut the screen on the living room window to climb into Joey's house. He found his brother at around 5:30 p.m., face down in bed. Immediately, he called 911.

"He was in the bed, the covers were pulled up about mid-back, and he was laying on the pillow with his arm up under him," said Shank Phelps, an Oktibbeha County Sheriff's Investigator. "He was facing the pillow, more or less."

"He'd been shot in the back of the head," added James Lindsey, an Oktibbeha County Sheriff's Constable.

**Building a case**

Chief investigator with the Oktibbeha County Sheriff's Department, Robert Elmore, was called in to process the scene of the homicide. After combing the house for possible evidence, he noticed that a section of living room carpet had the faint outline of a CPU, or a computer's central processing unit. He was unable to find Joey's wallet, or any shell casings left behind by the gun that had inflicted the fatal head wound.

Drawers were opened, and the house appeared to have been ransacked by home invaders.

"It actually looked like someone had come in and shot Joey in the back of the head, and then robbed the house of certain items," Robert said.

According to Robert's testimony, the home was equipped with security lights surrounding the perimeter – but he discovered that four bulbs had been unscrewed to keep them from turning on automatically. A latent-print examination was done by the Mississippi Crime Laboratory, which revealed a fingerprint belonging to Kristi Fulgham. Jason Pressley, who conducted the examination, testified that if the bulb had been on for an extended period of time, he wouldn't have been able to lift such a well-developed print – indicating that the bulbs had been unscrewed quite recently.

"Nothing I have heard has led me to believe that she was the kind of person who would expend the time or the effort it took to replace one of these security lights," said prosecutor Frank Clark at Kristi's trial, in response to a theory posited by the defense that the fingerprints were left after Kristi had done routine maintenance around the house.

"The testimony that I have heard over the past two days suggests that she would have waited for someone else – like Joey, or her brother Tyler – to do it for her."

An autopsy was performed on Joey's body by Dr. Steven Hayne, who testified that he located an entrance wound on the back of Joey's head, from which he extracted a small-caliber lead bullet. According to his testimony, the bullet was consistent with a .22 caliber projectile.

Dr. Hayne added that the cause of death was the gunshot wound that Joey had sustained, and estimated the time of death to have been approximately 36 to 48 hours before the body was discovered.

A .22 caliber weapon was missing from the home of Tyler Edmonds, Kristi's half-brother, according to Tyler's first cousin, Randy Simpson. Randy testified that he visited Tyler at his home on a regular basis – almost daily, he said. Prior to Joey's murder, there had been two .22 caliber weapons at Tyler's home, but the older weapon seemed to have disappeared. The weapon was a single-shot, bolt-action .22, Randy said, and Tyler – a lanky seventh grader – lacked the strength necessary to pull back the firing mechanism.

But according to Kristi and Tyler's biological father, Danny Edmonds, Kristi had been asking about a gun in the weeks leading up to Joey's death. According to Danny's testimony, Kristi said she "wanted Joey dead. That he (Joey) was mean to her and her kids." He added that she wanted him dead because she said, "he has a life insurance policy, and the kids would get $300,000 and I would get $200,000." And, as long as Danny "would keep his mouth shut," she said, she would buy him a Cadillac. According to Danny, he'd thought she was just kidding.

"Mr. Edmonds didn't tell law enforcement about it at the time, but once Joey was deceased, he went to the Sheriff's Department," Jim Waide said.

Vanessa Davis testified that Kristi had been asking her about guns, as well. About a month before Joey's body was found, Vanessa said Kristi had complained to her about a stray dog – and asked Vanessa to borrow her grandmother's gun, to shoot the dog. According to her testimony, Kristi asked for the gun three times, and seemed unwilling to take no for an answer.

She also testified that Kristi's attitude toward her husband wasn't typical of a woman intending to address her marital problems. When asked about the couple's relationship, Vanessa said they "were supposed to be getting back together and working things out," but when pressed by the State to clarify what exactly Kristi had told her, she responded, "that, you know, she was – it wasn't going to work out, basically."

Testimony was also obtained by Scotty Carrithers, who in 2003, had handled life insurance records for the National Guard unit stationed in Ackerman – Joey's unit. According to Scotty, Joey had taken out two life insurance policies. The first, in the amount of $55,000, listed Kristi as the beneficiary. The second policy, though, was worth $255,000.

Initially, the beneficiary named in the second policy was Kristi, as well – but Joey had updated the policy in 1999 and had changed the primary beneficiary to his mother. According to Scotty, Kristi didn't know. She'd called about a month before Joey's death, he said, inquiring about the amount of the policy. But Scotty hadn't been able to provide her with any information, since Joey had signed a privacy statement preventing Scotty from disclosing the details of the life insurance policy.

Kristi was arrested as soon as they got back from the coast – investigators had already spoken with her father and knew she'd been looking for a gun to get rid of her husband. And they'd already learned about the life insurance policy that Kristi had mistakenly assumed she was the beneficiary of.

Tyler's mother, Sharon Clay, was then asked by the investigators at the Oktibbeha County Sheriff's Office if she could bring her son in to answer a few questions. At the time, Sharon had no idea that Kristi had already told the authorities that Tyler had helped her commit the murder.

According to what Kristi had told police, Tyler had killed her husband unintentionally – by inadvertently discharging a rifle he'd been playing with. So they'd staged the scene, Kristi claimed, in an attempt to make the killing look like a robbery. And on their way down the coast, they disposed of the evidence – throwing the gun in a ditch along the highway.

"She said he was holding it up, pretending like he was going to shoot Joey, and the gun accidentally went off," said Tommy Whitfield.

**A false confession**

Tyler hardly seemed like the type to involved in anything so sordid. The story quickly spread throughout his hometown, and was soon picked up by national media – eventually, it was re-enacted on shows like "Blood Relatives" and "Snapped" and picked apart in minute detail on "Dr. Phil" and "Inside the Box."

Although in his initial interview, Tyler denied any participation in the shooting. He'd been waiting in the car with his sister's kids when the murder had happened, he said. He didn't even know Joey had been killed until two days later, when Kristi herself confessed to the police.

But he finally broke down when his mother was removed from the interview room and Kristi was allowed in to speak with him privately. The tactic is legal practice in murder cases in Mississippi, although other states have stricter regulations in place to reduce the likelihood of eliciting false confessions.

After speaking with Kristi, Tyler participated in a second, videotaped interview. Fidgeting, with his voice hushed, he told the detectives that together, he and his sister had pulled the trigger and killed her husband.

The interview hadn't even been going on for a half-hour before Sharon stormed into the room, demanding to know why the investigators were talking to her son without her present. But Tyler had already confessed. Sharon crouched down next to him, and – still on camera – Tyler sobbed and told her, "me and Kristi did it."

Later, Tyler said he'd been groomed by Kristi to provide the "right" answers. Before they were arrested, he said, she'd admitted to him that she'd shot her husband, and asked Tyler to deny her involvement if the police asked about it. If that didn't work, she added, she told him to tell them that he'd participated – that was the only way she could avoid receiving the death penalty, Tyler recalled. She had assured him, he said, that he wouldn't see any kind of serious punishment, since he was still a juvenile.

She was wrong, though. Tyler realized too late how serious his mistake was – he'd already been charged with murder.

Just four days after confessing to the detectives about his involvement in the killing, Tyler gave another recorded interview. In front of the camera, he told investigators that Kristi had put him up to it – she'd been the one to shoot Joey, while he sat in the car and waited for her. But that wasn't enough to convince prosecutors, or the jury.

In 2004, Tyler was convicted – based on those videotaped interviews and now-debunked testimony provided by a medical examiner, who claimed that the bullet wounds left on Joey Fulgham's body were consistent with two people having pulled the trigger simultaneously.

He was only 15 years old when he was sentenced to life behind bars, and became the youngest inmate at the notoriously harsh Walnut Grove Youth Correctional Facility – a privately-run centre that has since been closed.

**"Justice has finally been served."**
According to prosecutors, Kristi's motivation for killing her husband was completely financial – she wanted to steal whatever cash

she could, and hopefully cash in on a potential life insurance policy. But Kristi's lawyers presented another version of the events, arguing that the shooting was a desperate act of self-defence in an attempt to protect herself and her brother from a husband who had been abusing her. Kristi maintained that Tyler had helped her get rid of her husband.

Mitigation witnesses were called in during the sentencing phase, which provided the court with substantial background information about Kristi's past, as well as insight into her behaviour. According to psychiatrist Mark Webb, who performed an assessment of Kristi at Oktibbeha County Jail, Kristi "suffered from post-traumatic stress disorder and panic disorder with dependent personality traits."

This opinion, he explained, had been based on information provided by Kristi, including that she'd been raped by her biological father at the age of eleven; that one of her stepfathers, an alcoholic, had abused her mother; and that a different boyfriend of her mother's had intentionally neglected her.

Kristi's mother, Carol Morgan, supported some of these statements. She told the court that Kristi's biological father had been completely absent during her infancy, and refused to pay child support. She confirmed that she and Kristi had moved frequently, and that she'd been married and divorced several times – twice to abusive alcoholics. Also, she said, she had a variety of "male friends" who had lived with her and her daughter during Kristi's "formative years."

According to Sarah Ferguson, a long-time friend of Kristi's, said Kristi often stayed at her house when they were teenagers, because Kristi's father was "scary and mean." She added that she and Kristi had remained friends into adulthood, and testified that to her knowledge, Kristi was a good mother whose children were an important and valued part of her life.

A fourth mitigation witness, social worker Adrienne Dorsey-Kidd, was called to provide additional evidence pertaining to Kristi's character and background. However, the trial court barred Kristi's defense attorneys from presenting her testimony – which would have reflected that, in her review of Kristi's social history, Adrienne had determined that Kristi had lacked bonds with both her parents and had been exposed to substance abuse by both her mother and two different stepfathers.

Kristi was convicted in 2007. The jury determined that she was guilty of capital murder – killing her husband during the commission of a robbery for pecuniary gain – and unanimously found beyond a reasonable doubt that she had planned to use lethal force to eliminate her husband and steal his money and, potentially, a life insurance payout.

"Lastly, the jury unanimously found that the mitigating evidence did not outweigh the aggravating evidence," read the court documents, "and that Fulgham should suffer the penalty of death."

Just as she'd predicted.

The jury deliberated for just 58 minutes before stepping back into the courtroom and announcing Kristi's fate – death by lethal injection. Kristi sobbed loudly as the sentence was read by Circuit Clerk Angie McGinnis, and her mother, Carol, was fighting back tears of her own.

"Get away from me," she screamed at a photographer in the courtroom.

But not everyone was upset by the outcome – Joey Fulgham's family was pleased to hear the jury's verdict.

"I'm just so glad it's over with, and justice has finally been served," said Joey's mother, Ann Cash. "(The jury's deliberation) was quicker than I thought it would be – the District Attorneys did a terrific job, and I praise them. Joey can rest in peace now, and our family has peace of mind. I will pray that I can forgive Kristi one day."

Joey's brother, Shannon Fulgham, admitted the family had been waiting for years, "quietly and patiently," for Kristi to be found guilty of the crime she committed against his family.

"I tried not to look at her – just seeing her upsets me, after what she did to my brother," he said. "It's changed me and it's changed the way I look at life. I think she deserves the harshest punishment we can give to her, as citizens."

That same year, in 2007, the Mississippi Supreme Court threw out Tyler's conviction, claiming the testimony provided by that medical examiner should never have been allowed in court. The next year, a brand-new jury acquitted him.

According to Tyler's lawyer, Jim Waide, Kristi had manipulated Tyler – with the help of investigators looking to quickly wrap up a complicated case – into a false confession. All Tyler wanted, Waide said, was to do anything in his power to protect the half-sister he loved.

"He wasn't intending to go to jail for life," Waide told the Supreme Court, when Tyler was seeking compensation for the ordeal he suffered through. "That wasn't why he gave the false confession."

While Tyler said he struggled with a lot of guilt about what happened to him – and remains traumatized by the violence he experienced while at Walnut Grove, inflicted by both prisoners and guards – he doesn't feel embarrassed about it, anymore. In 2014, he moved to Florida, and now operates a commercial embroidery business.

"I'm an adult now, and I can look back and say, 'You were a kid. You did what probably nine out of ten kids would have done at the time.' And I can't go and change anything that happened," he said. "So, no, I'm not ashamed of it. And would say that the only regret I have is... I wish that I would have been as brave then as I am now."

In October of 2010, the Mississippi Supreme Court also overturned Kristi's death sentence, and another sentencing hearing was called for the 2003 murder conviction. The decision rested on the court's refusal to allow the testimony of Adrienne Dorsey-Kidd, the social worker. According to the Supreme Court's decision, there were no errors in the underlying conviction that led to the initial sentencing, but the trial court had "improperly barred" the witness' testimony.

At the time, prosecutors had argued that a social worker was ill-equipped to make official judgments about Kristi's psychology – and, according to the trial judge's determination, the opinion didn't offer anything beyond what a layperson might know.

"We find the trial court abused its discretion in refusing to allow Dorsey-Kidd to testify her opinions and observations after accepting her as an expert in the field of social work, and we are unable to say that such an error did not affect the jury's ultimate decision," wrote Justice Ann Lamar in the Supreme Court's decision.

Less than a month later, a new sentence was handed down by Oktibbeha County Circuit Court Judge Lee Howard – life in prison, with no possibility of parole.

# HUSBAND KILLER DONNA YAKLICH

## JESSI DIXON

## Old-fashioned police work

In December 1985, a narcotics detective was shot and killed in the driveway of his farm in Pueblo, Colorado, where he lived with his five children and his wife, Donna Yaklich. Initially, authorities suspected Dennis' death was linked to his work in law enforcement, but a tip led them to two teenage shooters – and eventually, back to Dennis' wife, Donna.

However, attorneys for Donna Yaklich argued that Dennis had been beating his wife. The murder, they claimed, was a battered woman's desperate attempt to escape a lifetime of abuse – or potentially becoming a murder victim herself, like Dennis' first wife, who is thought to have died of a diet drug overdose in 1977.

Yaklich was finally acquitted of first-degree murder after a mistrial and a second trial that has been described as "grueling," but was convicted on the charge of conspiracy for hiring gunmen to kill her husband. Her sentence was forty years in prison, but was released to a halfway house in 2005, after serving close to eighteen years.

The young men Yaklich had hired to carry out the murder were also arrested and sentenced. Charles Greenwell, who was only 16 when the crime was committed, received a sentence of twenty years while his brother Eddie, who had been 25, received thirty years.

However, while Yaklich's claims of abuse weren't enough to get her off on the premise of self-defence, they did encourage authorities to reopen their investigation into the death of Barbara Yaklich. According to a cold case team, the investigation was "incomplete."

"This case needed some good, old-fashioned police work," said team lead Steve Johnson, with the Colorado Bureau of Investigation. "In my opinion, I have seen better documented traffic accidents."

Discrepancies were found in the autopsy report, which originally claimed Barbara had fainted from taking diet pills. When her body-builder husband, Dennis, tried "energetically" to resuscitate her, she suffered bleeding in her abdomen. However, administering CPR is not an appropriate reaction to fainting – and as a police officer trained in CPR, Dennis would have known this.

Still, there was apparently no examination of the potential crime scene, and when Dennis was asked to take a polygraph to support his defense, he refused.

Denver-area pathologist Michael Doberson determined that the conclusions in the report were "very unusual" – the internal damage Barbara had suffered, he claimed, was more likely caused by a blow to the abdomen. Doberson included his findings in a letter to Johnson dated in 2005, stating that in his opinion, "the entire scenario is simply not credible." A second forensic pathologist concurred with Doberson's conclusions.

According to reports, Barbara's liver tore open and her abdomen was quickly filled with more than 2,000 millilitres of blood – nearly 40 per cent of her total blood volume, and more than twice as much as is typical in a victim of a fatal car accident.

Investigators are now considering her death as "suspicious," with the tear caused by a blunt force trauma consistent with "punches and knee drops to the upper abdomen," according to pathologist Stephen Cina. However, the autopsy report showed no other indications that would reveal a pattern of abuse – no recorded discoloration, bruising, or external signs of beatings.

While the investigation into Barbara's death is now complete, the case hasn't been closed. According to the coroner and the Pueblo County Sheriff, the public deserves answers to the questions that have been raised.

### The family man

Donna Yaklich met Dennis and his children only a few months after Barbara's death. According to Yaklich, the plan was to move in with the family for the summer and help him get the kids back into their home, since they were temporarily staying with Dennis' mother.

"I had no expected to fall in love with the children, who so desperately needed someone," Yaklich said. "They were grieving for their mother, so I couldn't bear to leave them."

Barbara had died on Valentine's Day, and had "appeared fine" as her children left for school that morning. However, an hour later, Barbara was dead – and Dennis was the only person who had been with her as she died. According to some reports, there are members of the community who do continue to question Dennis' involvement in the death of his first wife, including at least one of his former co-workers.

"Dennis' fellow officers knew he was out of control, but they also knew when they needed him he would be the first to go through the door," Yaklich said. "No one who worked with him would go against him."

It was this feeling of hopelessness that eventually led Yaklich to hire gunmen to kill her husband, in an effort to finally end the ongoing abuse. She'd moved in with Dennis when she was only 22 and he was 30. The children were aged 3, 9, 11, and 12 – and she immediately fell into the role of step-mother, despite the abuse which began only a month after Yaklich moved in. She said she attempted to leave a few times, but always went back.

"I feared Dennis, but at the same time I felt at home with him because I had grown up in an abusive environment," Yaklich said. "I fell into the trap of thinking if I could make everything perfect for him, he wouldn't get mad at me or at the kids. Dennis' threats to kill me or kill someone I loved if I ever left again kept me there."

Dennis even threatened to use his access to federal law enforcement agents against Yaklich, telling her that she'd never be able to get away from him – these agents were capable of fiding anyone, anywhere. Eventually, she said, "I lost myself. I lost hope."

"I became very depressed and mad at myself because I had no trusted my instincts about leaving the relationship when the abuse started," Yaklich said. "Suicidal thoughts became an answer. Then came homicidal thoughts."

Looking back, Yaklich admitted that she wished she had listened to those first instincts, but eventually came to a point where she no longer cared. However, she said she has been working on bettering herself since being convicted and sentenced.

"Being in prison is similar to the prison I put myself in while I was married to Dennis," she said. "However, prison is also what you make of it, so I've enrolled in educational programs, had therapy, and also taken care of myself. Things I should have done in society."

### A professional abuser

At a menacing 6'5" and 280 pounds, Dennis Yaklich was a competitive weightlifter who continuously used steroids to supplement his workouts – despite the fact that they also enhanced his aggressive tendencies. While the officers who worked with him conceded that he was always the go-to guy for breaking down a door or clearing a room, he was difficult to manage. In fact, when he did become confrontational, even a supervisor threatened to shoot him because they had no other way to defend themselves.

A former partner once stated that he felt he always had to "clean up after Dennis," and other co-workers have admitted they "dreaded" working with Dennis, because of his aggressive and unpredictable behaviour. Some of his closest colleagues have even confessed that Dennis displayed some "abusive tactics" on the job – while denying the complaints of citizens against him.

Yaklich endured what can only be described as domestic terrorism. While the physical abuse, which included slapping, choking, kicking, and pushing her down stairs as well as sadistic sexual assaults, was indeed disabling and troubling, the psychological abuse was almost worse. According to Yaklich, the threat of death loomed constantly – Dennis would put his gun to her head and threaten to kill her, point his finger at her in the shape of a gun and blow on it after miming shooting her with it, and even beating her under the cover of darkness so she wouldn't be able to prepare for the blows.

The physical abuse has been corroborated by a number of independent witnesses, including a mailman who reported seeing bruises on Yaklich's face, and a telephone repairman who had been called in twice to fix phones after Dennis had yanked them out of the wall in a fit of rage.

Following Yaklich's arrest, the repairman spoke with detectives investigating Dennis' death and said the bruises he had seen on Yaklich's neck and cheek were so prominent, he noticed them "at a glance." The detective inquired how the repairman could recall the incident so vividly, and he admitted that in his line of work, he sees "a lot of things like that in the low income areas and the projects, but I was shocked to see a cop's wife all bruised up like she was."

**Cries unheard**

Yaklich's first documented attempt for police intervention came in 1982, when she called Dennis' partner to explain that Dennis was "out of control" and threatening to kill her. The detective advised her to leave right away, but she said she was too afraid – if she left, she said, Dennis had told her he would kill her entire family, starting with her father.

Believing that Yaklich was in fear for her life, the detective immediately went to inform his supervisor about the call he'd received about his partner. According to the detective, the supervisor had gestured to indicate that he should just forget the call – it was none of their business – and the incident went unreported.

It was then that Yaklich realized that trying to get help from the police would be completely futile, and she would need to seek support elsewhere.

The next year, in November of 1983, Yaklich endured a short and traumatic visit with a psychologist. After Yaklich "sobbed uncontrollably" through the entire session, the psychologist recommended she leave her husband – but failed to offer her suggestions to muster the courage needed to do so, or what steps she could take to do it safely.

Since Yaklich was required to provide her abusive husband with detailed accounts of where she spent all her time, there was no way for her to continue therapy with regular appointments. She never went back for another session.

A few months later, Yaklich escaped to a battered women's shelter in Denver, in February of 1984. Dennis pleaded with her to come home, and even went so far as to promise that he would try to change – and because she was ashamed to go back to him again, Yaklich told the counselors that she was leaving the state.

Still, the abuse hadn't stopped another year later. Early in 1985, Yaklich tried talking to friends and family members – telling them she needed advice because Dennis was going to kill her. These claims were shrugged off by everyone she turned to, and the abuse began to escalate.

Feeling as though she had no other options, Yaklich began looking for an opportunity to kill herself. Her attempts failed, however, when she realized she would be abandoning her young son and step-children with their abusive father – and after witnessing the struggles of Barbara's children as they grieved the loss of their mother, she was unable to force that situation on her own child.

Later that year, the Pueblo Sheriff's Department received a 911 call from Yaklich's mother. One of the step-children had called Yaklich's parents after hearing what they thought was Dennis pushing Yaklich through a plate glass window. While it turned out that the noise was caused by just a bowl hitting the floor, the officers who responded barely acknowledged Yaklich.

In fact, their inspection of the situation involved a brief conversation with Dennis followed by a tour of the gym Dennis was building on the property. The situation only reinforced Yaklich's desperate situation on the other side of the blue line – living in fear of an abusive spouse with no support or protection from the authorities.

Finally, on December 12, 1985, one of Yaklich's friends finally responded to her pleas for help. A neighbour, Eddie Greenwell, waited at the Yaklich family's farm with his younger brother, Charles, into the early morning hours. When Dennis returned home after working a night shift, the brothers shot and killed him. Yaklich was inside the house, sleeping.

According to court documents, Yaklich had "approached several people" in an attempt to have her husband killed, and had met with Eddie Greenwell many times over a period of eight months. The Greenwell brothers were paid $4,200 in installments after the murder was committed – although the brothers testified they had been promised $45,000.

The story of the tragic marriage was detailed in a made-for-television movie called *Cries Unheard: The Donna Yaklich Story*. The film was released in 1994 and starred former Charlie's Angel Jaclyn Smith as Yaklich.

### A disturbing conflict of interest

After Dennis was killed, the Pueblo Police Department – Dennis' employer – carried out an investigation into his death, despite the fact that the murder actually took place in the jurisdiction of the Pueblo Sheriff's Office. Lead roles in the inquiry were awarded to narcotics detectives – Dennis' partners.

The District Attorney was also a personal friend of Dennis', and even admitted to being a material witness in his own case. At the time of the trial, DA Sandstrom was wrapped up in a highly contested election – and this clear political agenda, combined with the attempts of the police department to hide its role in Yaklich's abuse and ultimately, Dennis' death, indicate incredible prejudice against Yaklich from the very beginning.

Not that Yaklich was surprised. After attempting to secure the help of police several times during the course of her abusive marriage, it was obvious to Yaklich that law enforcement was not on her side.

Still, the jury acquitted Yaklich of the charge of first-degree murder. Several jurors even thought Yaklich deserved to be acquitted of all charges, but felt intimidated by the Pueblo Police Department – and feared potential retaliation. Instead, the jury voted guilty on the charge of conspiracy to commit murder, believing that the fair-minded judge would give the battered wife the minimum sentence of eight years.

The probation supervisor who had conducted Yaklich's pre-sentencing investigation testified that Yaklich would be an "excellent candidate" for sentencing alternatives outside of the Department of Corrections, and gave the court his recommendation for the minimum sentence. His testimony affirmed the sense of desperation Yaklich claimed to be struggling with.

"I really felt that whether they did what she wanted done, to have Dennis killed, or whether Dennis found out and killed her, it didn't matter," he said. "She was at a point in her life where either was satisfactory."

However, the late Judge Seavy who presided over the trial chose to overlook the circumstances leading to Dennis' murder and remanded Yaklich to the Department of Corrections for a sentence of forty years. According to the judge, Yaklich "started this whole scenario," and therefore deserved to serve a period of time "in excess of the longest Greenwell's sentence."

"We cannot overlook the fact that Yaklich's participation in the death of her husband was not merely peripheral," stated court documents. "Had it not been for Yaklich, the Greenwells would not have been involved in this murder. Thus, in our view, we would be establishing poor public policy if Yaklich were to escape punishment by virtue of an unprecedented application of self-defense while the Greenwells were convicted of murder."

Still, the jurors were shocked and horrified by the severity of Judge Seavy's harsh sentence. More than half of the serving jurors submitted letters expressing their disappointment with the resulting sentence to a judge who presided over Yaklich's sentencing reconsideration a few years later. These letters were dismissed by that judge, however, who felt "that they must not allow for personal sympathy to influence their decision." Several of the jurors who served on the initial trial event went on to diligently advocate for Yaklich's early release, eighteen years later.

According to Dr. Lenore Walker, who counseled and evaluated Yaklich and provided expert testimony at her trial, Judge Seavy was "using the court and a woman's life to express his own ignorance of a battered woman's plight."

**The conspiracy**

According to court documents, Yaklich did receive payments totalling more than $250,000 under her late husband's three life insurance policies – leading to a theory that the motivation that pushed her to arrange her husband's death was to obtain this insurance money. The defense argued that Yaklich suffered from "battered woman syndrome," and that the conspiracy to commit murder was a "justifiable act of self-defence ... committed under duress resulting from years of physical and psychological battering by her husband."

"Yaklich lived in a constant state of fear of her husband," the defense argued. "At the time of his death, she believed she was in imminent danger of being killed by him or receiving great bodily injury from him."

The defense went on to explain that many battered women are unable to safely leave their abusive spouses – and in fact, the abuse often escalates as a result of a separation. Abusers have also been known to pursue their victims after they've left, subjecting them to "brutal attacks."

"Additionally, battered women may not psychologically or emotionally have the alternative of leaving the abuser because of their low self-esteem, their emotional and economic dependency, the absence of another place to go, and the woman's legitimate fear of the abuser's response to her leaving," stated the defense. "Battered women become trapped in their own fear and often feel that their only recourse is to kill the batterer or be killed."

Several people involved with the case, including District Attorney Sandstrom, have stated that if Yaklich had gone ahead and committed the murder herself, "she would have walked." However, the DA and many others also question the validity of Yaklich's testimony, including that Dennis was abusing her – maintaining the theory that Yaklich conspired to have him killed just to receive the insurance money.

The DA even stated that "if she had shot him herself, there would be no issue" – leading some to wonder if Sandstrom sees money as an acceptable motive for murder, as long as you follow through with it on your own.

Like most battered women, Yaklich both loved and hated her husband. Killing him herself would have been difficult, as she was afraid that as soon as she pointed a gun at him to save herself and her children, the love she had for him would "override her fear of him," and cause her to second-guess her decision. The ramifications from that could have bene deadly.

Another concern for Yaklich was her husband's established persona of invincibility – one he had carefully instilled in her over years of repeated psychological and physical abuse. Not only did Yaklich struggle to trust in her own ability to kill her husband, she struggled to believe that he would ever really die.

One of the prosecution's expert witnesses, Dr. Alice Brill, said in her testimony that Yaklich didn't meet the traditional profile of a battered woman. These women, according to Brill, generally kill their spouses with little premeditation and show little interest in pursuing relationships with other men – while Yaklich spent at least ten months planning her husband's murder, and had had at least one extramarital affair about a year before Dennis was killed.

Dennis' children also continue to question Yaklich's testimony, stating that none of them had ever witnessed any physical abuse from Dennis during the eight years of the couple's marriage. After Yaklich's parole hearing in October 2005, Dennis' daughter Vanessa fought back tears while talking about the court's decision to release Yaklich after she'd only served eighteen years of her forty-year sentence.

"It's devastating – I don't believe justice has prevailed," she said. "My father died at age 38. He was stripped of his opportunity to live life. He was prevented from raising his children, from seeing us grow up and accomplishing our goals."

Vanessa stated that Yaklich's claims of beatings and abuse were "an outright lie" – and that the depiction of the family's life shown in the TV-movie *Cries Unheard* were based entirely on prison interviews with Yaklich herself, with no supporting evidence or facts contributed by other relatives or friends.

Vanessa added that just two months before her father was killed, Yaklich had told her that Dennis had asked for a divorce – but that the couple planned to delay the proceedings until after the Christmas holidays, for the sake of the younger children. This story has been corroborated by Dennis' brother, who said Dennis told him over the phone that he planned to divorce Yaklich once the holidays had passed.

"(Dennis') life was taken because he was going to divorce my step-mother and not because she was the victim of abuse," Vanessa said. "I never feared my father, nor did I observe any abuse, whether it be psychological or physical, perpetrated by him. His demeanor was calm and loving, his words encouraging and supportive. I can honestly state my step-mother did not provide my siblings or myself with the same."

According to Vanessa, Yaklich didn't show any grief or remorse after Dennis had been killed – and even slapped Vanessa when she began to cry at her father's funeral. She went on to detail the ongoing "injustice," claiming to defend her father since he is no longer able to defend himself.

"My stepmother's legal defense was paid for by my father's life insurance proceeds and my family and I believe she profited from the made-for-television monstrosity," Vanessa said. "Most recently, her financial status has provided her with the ability to hire a media publicist."

Questions also remain about the relationship Yaklich had with her defense attorney, John Giduck. Records show Giduck and Yaklich took a romantic vacation to Jamaica together prior to her arrest in March 1986 – a getaway funded entirely from the death benefit Yaklich received after having her husband murdered.

In fact, the vacation was cut short when Yaklich was notified of the charges that were being brought against her, and surrendered to police upon her return to Pueblo. Most of the insurance money had already been spent by the time Yaklich was arrested.

According to information reported in the Colorado Springs Gazette, Yaklich had been involved in an extramarital affair about a year before Dennis' murder, and had begun a romantic relationship with Giduck only weeks after her husband's death. Giduck had apparently attended Dennis' funeral, where he had given Yaklich his business card and told him to call if she needed anything.

Yaklich reached out to him a few days later, after police asked her to verify the statement she'd given with a routine polygraph test.

### A safe and abuse-free life

Still, Yaklich had a spotless record prior to her incarceration, which continued even after she was sent to prison – a testament to her strength of character. According to prison records, Yaklich managed to vigilantly avoid conflict and strictly followed the many rules surrounding prison life. Despite being forced into an environment filled with trouble, Yaklich managed to stay out of it through her entire eighteen-year term.

During her incarceration, Yaklich obtained an associate's degree as well as a Bachelor's degree in psychology – while working in maintenance and then in a computer-refurbishing program at the correctional facility. According to staff there, Yaklich was a hard and industrious worker, even volunteering her time as a member of the Fire Response Team, comprised of prisoners trained in firefighting and first aid.

Yaklich has also volunteered with several programs that support victims of abuse, earning high praise from her Department of Corrections supervisors regarding the effectiveness of her work with young people. She encourages victims of domestic abuse to seek support from therapy groups to find the strength to break away from an abusive partner – to learn how to stay away emotionally and physically.

"Educating ourselves about the issues and statistics relative to domestic violence will help us pass this information on to the next generation," Yaklich said. "Our children need to learn that they have the right to safe and abuse-free lives."

# HUSBAND KILLER JANE DOROTIK

## ANNA MICHAELS

Murder at the Charisma Ranch

Robert Dorotik was born in 1945, two years before his future wife Jane Marguerite Colvey. It would be 23 years before they would meet and fall in love. They married on April 4, 1970 in Los Angeles California.

Two years later Nicholas was born, another son Alexander would follow shortly after that and by January 16, 1976 their family would be complete with the birth of their daughter Claire Elizabeth.

Robert was an Engineer and Jane was a Health care professional as well as a successful business woman. She made a six figure salary from her 9-5 job alone, and the horse ranch she ran with her daughter was starting to bring in money too.

Robert and Jane would have more than one argument over the money Jane and their daughter Claire spent on Charisma Ranch. He quit his job as an engineer to support Jane's endeavor of raising and training horses. Bob started a business making horse jumps, but by 2000 his business was in trouble. One of the last arguments Jane and Bob had was when Jane and Claire told him they found another horse that would be perfect for the ranch. Robert complained they didn't need any more horses. This infuriated Jane and she told him in no uncertain terms that it was her money and she would spend it how she wanted, she didn't need his permission.

On the afternoon of February 13, 2000 Jane got ready to go down to tend to the horses. Bob was dressing in his jogging clothes and told Jane he was going to go for a run. Bob had been a long distance runner for years. Jane had an injury that prevented her from participating. Jane asked her husband to stoke the fire before he left and she went to the barn.

Mrs. Dorotik returned to the house a couple hours later and Bob was nowhere to be found. She waited a while longer and began looking for him. There were others including neighbors and sons Nick and Alex. Becoming increasingly worried about her husband Jane called the police and told them that he had not come home after his run. A search was organized by the police and in the early morning hours of February 14, 2000 Police found Robert's battered, bloodied body by the side of the road about three miles from home. Police immediately suspected Jane.

Robert Dorotik had died from blunt force trauma and strangulation. He had several injuries to the face and the back of the head (an expert testified the wounds were consistent with a hammer). There were defensive wounds on his hands. He was still wearing his jogging clothes although according to the detectives his shoes were tied in an odd manner. The rope used to strangle him was still around his neck and had made a laceration on his throat.

They did not find blood at the scene that would have been consistent with it being the murder site. Robert had been killed somewhere else and moved here. They found the tire tracks and shoe prints. Jane could not be linked to any of the shoe prints, only the tire tracks. However, hers were not the only tire tracks there, the others were not linked to anyone.

The evidence from the beginning seemed to point at Jane Dorotik as the killer. At the scene where they found the body there were tire tracks that matched the three different treads on her truck. At the residence there was a massive amount of blood that had been cleaned at. Jane claims that the blood was from a nosebleed Robert had and cleaned up. Between the box springs and mattress there was a towel soaked with blood. In a bag in the master bedroom they found a syringe with a horse tranquilizer in it and Jane's fingerprint in Bob's blood was found on it. She was arrested before the blood analysis could even be returned.

Around the room investigators found impact blood spatter patterns as well as drip, transfer and cast off. In one of the closets in the house they found a steam carpet shampooer and a significant amount of cleaning supplies. Bob's blood was found on the cap, handle and nozzle of one of the bottles.

Blood stains consistent with Robert's were found in the bed of the truck Jane, Claire and the ranch hands used around the ranch. They found no blood spatter on his shoes or shirt, but did find some blood on his boxers. One of the two hands never showed up for work the day after Bob's death.

Jane was booked into San Diego County Jail and with the help of family made bail.

Jane's daughter Claire was incriminated in the murder, that she was actually the one that killed Robert, her own father. It was well known that father and daughter had a stormy relationship, and at times became volatile. It was never revealed why the two seemed to hate each other, but Claire even wrote a scathing letter to her father about a "betrayal of trust."

Jane's defense team Kerry Steigerwalt and Cole Casey now had to figure out how to defend their 55 year old client. What they decided on wasn't the most unusual way to do it and it and many other attorneys had done in numerous courtrooms around the country. They deliberately brought Claire up as a suspect. By showing that another person 'could' have committed the murder there is a chance that it will raise enough of a doubt in a jury's mind for them to bring back an acquittal instead of a guilty verdict. This is what the attorney's for Jane were doing, trying to raise a reasonable doubt. This strategy would ultimately tear the family apart. In a letter written three years after her conviction Jane would call her attorney 'ego driven' and the implicating of her daughter a 'seriously flawed defense strategy.'

Prosecutor Bonnie Howard-Regan was convinced that Jane killed her husband to keep from having to pay him spousal support. It seemed there was an impending divorce on the horizon for Bob and Jane. They had separated in 1997 but talked it out and decided to keep their money separate and got back together.

Their own sons commented that their parents' marriage wasn't the most loving and at times their fights became very heated. But is this a motive for murder? Perhaps not just the fights, maybe it was the fact that if the two divorced Jane would have to pay Robert up to 40% of her annual income. This would be upwards of 50,000 dollars a year. Jane was incensed when a divorce attorney had told her that. That is a huge motive for murder in the eyes of the law. There was also a $250,000 life insurance policy on both Bob and Jane. She was forthcoming with the detectives about this during the investigation. If she had to pay that much out in spousal support she wouldn't be able to keep the horse ranch, and it seemed that was all she cared about.

Jane's trial would begin in May of 2001 a little over a year after her husband was murdered. Jane had pled not guilty and was making passionate pleas to the public declaring her innocence. Though her daughter and sister also claimed that Jane was innocent of this heinous crime, Claire, Bonnie Long and a ranch hand all invoked their Fifth Amendment right against self-incrimination. Steigerwalt brought up the fact that Claire's alibi was never confirmed. Had the Sheriff's Department zeroed in on Jane in a hasty attempt to close the case?

On June 9, 2001 the case of Jane Dorotik v The State of California went to the jury for deliberation. After the third day both the defense and the prosecution were starting to worry. Maybe they hadn't presented their case as well as they'd thought. Maybe they didn't explain things in an easy to understand way. In the end however, it wasn't that the jury had a problem understanding what they saw and heard during the trial. They were just being diligent, making sure every juror understood what the evidence was and how it fit in the scheme of things. In fact, they had a unanimous decision on the first vote...guilty on the charge of first degree murder.

Judge Joan Weber said that there was "an overwhelming amount of circumstantial evidence" and when Jane's attorney filed for a new trial it was denied. New witnesses had come forward and Steigerwalt asked that the case be reopened to the jury could hear what they had to say. She denied his request. Weber also asked, "How could you have your husband's blood on your hands if you had nothing to do with his death?" The Judge Weber was referring to the syringe with Janes fingerprint on it. It was an integral piece of evidence in the case.

Without a new trial in San Diego County, the next step is Court Of Appeal Of California, Fourth Appellate District, Division One.

The Court of Appeals works differently than the Trial Court. It is not a place for a new trial or a retrial. They won't look at new evidence or hear from new witnesses. It is strictly for trying to overturn the lower court's decision. If this happens then the Trial Court would be made to do one of several different actions in the case. One would be a whole new trial, which in Jane's case is what her attorney would want to happen. Or perhaps the Appellate Court would order Trial Court to look at additional evidence and/or revisit the facts in the case.

Either of these would be a win for Jane and her defense team. However, before these could happen her attorney would have to show that there was an error in the trial procedure or in how Weber interpreted the law.

This all starts with a Notice to Appeal, and then a brief has to be filed. In many cases appeals are decided based solely on this brief. Other times there will oral arguments before anything is decided.

Janes appeal was filed on November 18, 2003. She is asserting that Judge Weber should have included in the instructions to the jury the lessor charge of voluntary manslaughter because the state didn't present evidence that there was premeditation and aforethought to constitute first degree murder. She was denied.

On June 12, 2009 Jane filed another appeal. There were three key facts in this appeal. In the first one she claims 'ineffective assistance of counsel'. Jane claimed that her defense team didn't represent her properly. They didn't do any investigation of their own.

Second, she believed that not letting the jury hear from the new witnesses and not doing DNA testing jeopardized her case. The rope used to strangle Robert was never test for DNA, claiming that epithelia's of the real killer would have been found.

Third, there were procedural mistakes because of the delayed discovery and her actual innocence.

The defense was not allowed to present evidence that the State's expert witness had many mistakes in other cases by using 'faulty methodology'. The jury was not allowed to hear from an eyewitness.

The Appellate Court denied her, again.

The San Diego Union-Tribune reported on November 22, 2015 that a Judge has determined Jane be allowed to have the DNA in her case tested. The rope used to strangle Bob, the fingernail scrapings, and a piece of hair found around the victim's finger all be tested.

Jane still proclaims her innocence and said the ranch hand that didn't show up for work the day after the murder should be considered. He drives a black pick-up, and his tire tracks were also found at the scene. She also reiterated that the man owed the Dorotik's money.

Jane filed her first appeal on November 18, 2003. The Appellate court upheld the lower court's decision. Then Jane, known also as the petitioner filed Habeas petition on April 4, 2006 in the State Superior Court. Next was a Habeas Petition in the Appellate Court on January 3, 2006. And again Jane filed with the State Supreme Court on November 20, 2006. All appeals and motions to this point had been denied or affirmed the lower court's decision.

On June 1, 2007 Jane would file a Petition for Writ of Habeas Corpus, a Motion to appoint counsel, a Motion for Leave to Proceed in Forma Pauperis and a request for DNA testing. This too was denied or dismissed.

In July of 2007 Jane managed to get the money for filing fees and Magistrate Judge Porter ordered the case be reopened on July 9, 2007.

In the appeal for ineffectual assistance of counsel the superior court "denied the claims on the merits in a written order but only addressed the first two claims. On appeal the Appellate Court did the same thing.

Jane contends that council should have done independent testing of the forensic evidence that the prosecution would be presenting at trial and that there was other available evidence that he could have taken advantage of but didn't. Jane contends that had he done so the findings would have weakened the prosecution's case.

Another point the petitioner brought up is that her counsel didn't call her as a witness in her own defense.

Petitioner wanted a medical professional called as an expert witness to testify as to the medical impossibility that she could have perpetrated the murder due to an injury from an accident years earlier. That she would not have had the strength to do what the prosecution says she did.

Counsel for the defense did not object when a detective testified that he thought she was the killer. He could have also asked for a mistrial also.

He didn't insist on DNA testing prior to the start of the trial, armed with the results of the tests, petitioner is sure that it would have pointed to the real killer or killers.

Petitioner believes that her counsel should have brought up different scenarios that could have explained away the circumstantial evidence brought up at trial.

That he could have provided innocent theories for the incriminating evidence.

He didn't show that police didn't follow any leads, including eyewitnesses that came forward in the early stages of the investigation; they made up their mind that she was guilty. Therefore they didn't look for the real killer/killers.

Jane contends that her counsel could have done their own investigation and found the witnesses that were not heard at trial. Instead he made the leap to blaming Claire Dorotik as a defense.

And finally, follow through on the promises counsel made to the jury about what the evidence would show, and not make a comment to the affect that Jane was guilty.

If none of these ten points were true but the last one, would that fact that her own defense counsel made a comment that directly or indirectly told the jury he thought she was guilty should have been grounds for a mistrial and perhaps proceedings started to disbar her attorney.

The points brought up in Jane's eyes caused her to be wrongly convicted for the murder of her husband.

The forensic evidence in many parts does not support the prosecution's theory. Think about the "blood" found on the wall that supposedly dripped down from the master bedroom upstairs. The man who sold /rented the property to the Dorotik's knew of a water leak. Rain water would get in the track of the sliding door and seep down the wall of the stairs leading to the bedroom. There was Bob's DNA there, but was it from blood? Walking shirtless up the stairs and rubbing his sweaty arm on the wall could leave his DNA, it was not said that it was blood.

Post-conviction reports showed that there was way less blood present than would have been if the State's expert witness, Merrit, were correct. McDonell who did the post-conviction report says the fatal blow probably occurred outside the bedroom. But at the same time doesn't accept the idea that Bob was killed where he was found or that he was killed somewhere else, body dumped where it was found and the blood evidence planted.

McDonell also said that the blood on the mattress could have easily been caused by a bloody nose. That being said it still doesn't explain the different blood stain patterns found throughout the room. Those where found on the pillow, nightstand, walls, bedspread and the window. Those he said cannot be explained away by a nosebleed.

The post-conviction report says that Merrit's testimony was wrong inasmuch as there was not enough blood soaked in to support his idea that Bob remained on the mattress for a long time after the attack.

McDonell concurs with petitioner that the blood around the pot-belly stove could very well have been from the nosebleed. Petitioner wants further testing to find out if it even had anything to do with the murder at all.

The bloody thumb print on the syringe was due to Bob helping Jane with a vet procedure. There was a horse tranquilizer inside the syringe and Jane's thumbprint in Bob's blood on it. This was admitted into evidence? Why, it's said to be a 'key piece' of evidence in the prosecution's case. Petitioner's counsel didn't object? Per Bob's toxicology report there was no drugs in his system. How did they tie it into the murder?

The truck, tire tracks and shoe prints. There was much to do about the tire tracks at the scene where Bob's body was found. There were actually two sets, one belonging to the family truck, the one that everyone including the farm hands had access to. But there was another set, never identified. The shoe prints found also at the scene couldn't be attributed to Jane either. Both sets were too big. The tracks that showed Jane's truck had backed up at the spot where the body was found can easily be explained as well. Bob used the truck to measure jogging routes. If he were to come to the exact length he wanted, he would have just turned around at that spot, hence the backup tracks.

A cursory search of the house was done the evening that Jane reported Bob missing. Police and Police dogs were all in the house including the master bedroom. They didn't find any blood.

Jane was in an accident in 1983 and had a severe injury to a hip which had to be put back together with metal and screws. The prosecution says that Jane would have bludgeoned her husband, then carried him down the stairs from the bedroom, through the house, across a 60' porch and lifted him into the back of a full sized Ford

F250. Defense counsel should have brought up the fact that his client couldn't have done any of that. The Appellate court says that her sons saw her pulling irrigation pipes around the ranch that weighed about 75 lbs. pulling on 75lbs of something is different than lifting 147 lbs of dead weight.

Detective Richard Empson when questioned about the rope used to strangle Robert Dorotik and why it wasn't tested for DNA said the "criminologists in his office discouraged testing it because too many people had handled it." When pressed about the possibility of DNA on it that could have belonged to Claire or the ranch hand Leonel Morales or someone else and lead to the real killer, what then? Empson continued, "I believe I know who killed Bob Dorotik, that's why I arrested Jane Dorotik." Personal opinions are not supposed to be brought in to testimony, especially from an officer of the court. Did Jane's counsel object to this? Did it prejudice the jury against the petitioner? It could be said that it inflamed the jury. Most jurors will believe a law enforcement officer over anyone else. Even if the comment was objected to and stricken from the record the juror's still heard it and no matter if they are told to disregard it, it will still be in their mind.

There are so many points that Jane brought up on each one of her appeals. And each and every one of them were dismissed by the Courts. Many of Jane's friends and family still believe that Jane is innocent and should at least get a new trial so all of the evidence can be heard and that maybe she can even testify in her own defense. Although her trial court attorney believed that doing so was not a good idea. Clearly he didn't believe his client was innocent of the crime.

In the findings of the Appellate Court they say that the petitioner didn't show how not having the jury hear that Merrit's methodology was flawed and that he had been wrong on other cases would not have changed the jury's verdict.

They stated that even though the petitioner believes that the prosecution purposefully did not test for DNA she cannot prove how it would have changed anything. Also added the testing would not have brought forth any exculpatory or impeaching evidence. Knowing that DNA has set wrongfully convicted people free by proving their innocence this statement seems wrong in its entirety. Jane would be in a Catch 22 scenario, she can't prove that by not testing there was an error in law and without being able to prove it would help her case they wouldn't allow the testing.

Jane says she's been through a living hell since being sent to Chowchilla's prison facility in central California. But she hasn't been wasting her time. Along with filing the above mentioned appeals she is fighting for her fellow prisoners who are over the age of 55.

Jane is appalled at how many women are incarcerated and how the number keeps growing every year. She was once a mental health professional and says that a large number of women in prison should be in a Mental Health facility.

According to Jane "Medical care is liken to a third world country." And "there are women dying in prison alone and unnoticed by prison staff.

What she is trying to get done is this, have more compassionate releases, the parole board has the authority to do this but won't. So a program is working its way through legislation in the state of California. "If The Risk Is Low, Let Them Go".

Jane isn't advocating opening the flood gates and letting these women head off to parts unknown. There are a certain set of criteria in place to make sure the risk is actually low.

First of all, they have to have served at least 50% of their sentence or seven years.

They can't have had any disciplinary actions in the past five years. In other words they have to be a model prisoner.

They cannot have any other felony convictions of their record and they must have a concrete, safe place to stay in the community

These are safeguards to keep reoffenders inside the prison walls. Jane is very passionate about this program. She has watched many of what she calls "Golden Girls" languishing with terminal illnesses for years, alone, not able to be with family because Chowchilla houses inmates from all over the state.

Many of the families just don't have the money or time to be able to travel to see their loved ones. And even the children have to be patted down before they can go in to see a relative, to possibly say a last goodbye.

Jane's alternative custody program has to clear through law makers and with the help of different advocates it's headed in the right direction thanks to Carol Lui a senator from California.

This is being heralded as a great program to help with overcrowding of the prisons in California, and if this comes about in a timely manner it could help Jane as well. She is now 68 years old.

# HUSBAND KILLER : THE TRUE STORY OF KELLY GISSENDANER

42

## JENNIFER KENDALL

Kelly Gissendaner, born Kelly Brookshire, became the sixth and last woman executed in Georgia for her role in the murder of her husband, Douglas Gissendaner, by her lover, Greg Owen. The murder was gruesome, Kelly demonstrated a lack of credibility with lies, and the murder was clearly premeditated- three things that helped a jury convict her of her role in the murder. What hurt her the most, though, was that her former lover turned on her and testified against her. Kelly seemingly changed her life in prison, mentoring and preaching to other women. Her legal team appealed the decision due to a lack of proof, her redemption, and her relationship with her children. The mother of three children cried and sang "Amazing Grace" as she received the lethal injection and one hundred people protested her death outside.

**Early Life**

In 1968, Kelly Brookshire was born to Maxine and Marry Brookshire in Georgia. She has a brother that was born one year after Kelly. Kelly and her brother were not born into wealth or emotional stability. Her family consisted of simple cotton farmers. Her parents drank, did drugs, and fought. Due to the troubled relationship, they did not stay together. Kelly's father left the family and created a new one with no intention of including Kelly into his new family dynamic. This obviously left Kelly feeling unwanted and abandoned. Kelly's mother did remarry a man named Billy Wade eight days after the divorce with Kelly's father was final, but Billy only added more trauma to Kelly's already broken home. Many people came forward with knowledge of sexual abuse to Kelly by her stepfather and other men. On top of the sexual abuse, Billy Wade was physically and emotionally abusive to Kelly, her brother, and her mother. Luckily, her mother also divorced Billy Wade and moved the family.

Kelly stood at six feet tall, and she was rather homely looking. Many people made fun of her for her looks and being "trailer trash". She would prefer to work rather than socialize, mostly due to her household's financial situation and her mother's strict rules. Her first job was at McDonald's. She mostly kept to herself, but the outcast made one friend in a woman named Mitzi.

### First child and marriage

Kelly got pregnant with her first child before she finished high school. She claimed that the child was conceived through date rape, and the father was not actively involved in the child's life. She refused to name the father to even her best friends. She also tried to hide the pregnancy for as long as she could, but the reality became apparent around her sixth month. Before she gave birth, her father reached out to her and suggested that she name the child with his last name. Her first child, Brandon Brookshire, was born in June of 1986. Kelly married her first husband, Jeff Banks, at the young age of nineteen, but the marriage only lasted for six months before it dissolved. Reports indicate that the marriage quickly ended when Kelly's father threatened Jeff with a gun for not passing him bread at the dinner table. After the marriage ended, Kelly and her baby moved into her mother's trailer. This was a rough time for Kelly, but she was saved when she met Douglas Gissendaner.

### Marriage to Douglas Gissendaner

On September 2, 1989, Kelly became Mrs. Douglas Gissendaner... for the first time. Kelly was four months pregnant on her wedding day, which could have encouraged the nuptials. The marriage was tumultuous from the beginning. They had financial difficulty after they both lost their jobs and were forced to live with Doug's parents for some time. However, Doug provided a good life for Kelly and her child when he decided to enlist in the United States Army. Despite a steady paycheck, Kelly used the money irresponsibly and needed Doug's family to help her with car payments. Doug's parents already didn't love Kelly, and this added to their distrust. When Doug moved to Germany because of his job in the army, it only added to the tension. The move happened only one month after Kelly had given birth to their first child together and her second child, Kayla. When Kelly and Doug were together, they were noticeably miserable. The relationship did not work at all, and they fought constantly. People also spoke up about Kelly's partying and sleeping around with other men while Doug wasn't around. This caused even more strain on the family, and the couple divorced in 1993. This time, Kelly joined the army with no other way to support herself and her children, but she discovered that she was not made for the army. During this time, Kelly became pregnant with another man and gave birth to her final child Jonathan who everyone called Cody. This father would die of cancer shortly after his birth. After returning from the army, Kelly and Doug reconciled. Despite having a child with another man, they didn't want to separate their family. They remarried in May of 1995 and, despite a separation during this time, bought a house together in Auburn, Georgia in December of 1996. A few months later, Doug was murdered.

**Greg Owen**

While divorced from Doug, Kelly started working for the International Readers League of Atlanta. At this time, she started socializing with her boss, Belinda Owens. When she met Belinda's brother Greg Owen, they had an instant chemistry. The relationship started strong, but it soon started to worry Belinda. Belinda noticed an alarming amount of fighting, and she didn't appreciate the bossy tone that Kelly used when she spoke to her brother. Kelly and Greg broke up, and Kelly went back to Doug and remarried. Kelly and Greg rekindled their romance during a brief separation between Kelly and Douglas, but Kelly ultimately stayed married to Douglas. Many suspect her devotion to her relationship with Doug involved stability for her and her children rather than love. This was only amplified by the fact that many reports indicated that she continued to maintain a relationship with Owen throughout her marriage to Douglas.

**Murder and Investigation**

In February 7, 1997, Douglas Gissendaner was murdered by in a secluded part of rural Gwinnett County. Douglas came home from a friend's house shocked to find Gregory Owen in his home. Gregory then exhibited a knife and forced Douglas to drive to a remote area. When they stopped, Owen forced Douglas out of the car and made him walk 300 feet into the woods before beating him in the skull with a nightstick and repeatedly stabbing him in the neck and back. When Kelly arrived, she helped set the car on fire to eliminate any evidence.

The night of the murder, Kelly had gone out for dinner and drinks with friends. Despite dancing and having a good time, she went home right around midnight. Friends with her that night reported that she told them that she went home because she had a feeling that there was something wrong. Kelly frantically searched for Doug when he didn't come home the next day. She made several calls, but she reportedly could not locate him. She even called his parents to ask if they had seen him. That same day a missing person's report was created by the local police department, and they started their search immediately.

Investigators had trouble with Kelly's story from the start. When she spoke with them, she described her marriage as happy and noneventful, but other people provided reports of fighting and numerous problems including Kelly's infidelity. One name that came up over and over again in interviews with friends and family was Greg Owen.

Greg Owen seemed to have a reasonable alibi. A roommate stated that he was home all night and got picked up by a friend for work the following morning at 9:00 a.m. With his roommate's alibi, police put Greg's interrogation on hold and continued their investigation.

Investigators finally got a big clue when they found Doug's car. It was left on a rural road in Gwinnett County. The most interesting thing about finding the car was that it appeared to be burned from the inside. At this time, there was no sign of Doug. While the situation didn't look good for Doug, family and friends knew that police were getting closer to the truth.

The day that the car was found, friends and family gathered to the home of Doug Sr. and Sue Gissendaner to support them during this difficult time. Kelly made an appearance, but she didn't stay long. She decided instead to take her children to the circus. While some people can understand how the environment can be traumatic to the children and maybe Kelly wanted to protect them, people found her decision evasive and questionable. Also, shouldn't the children be allowed to mourn with their grandparents? To increase suspicion even more, Kelly went back to work only four days into the search for her missing husband. Her behavior confused people around her. Sure, she had bills to pay, but four days was very soon to go back to work. Many people thought that she was hiding something. Many more people reported a weird attitude for a woman who had a missing husband.

After an already excruciating twelve days for Doug's friends and family, Doug's body was finally found in a horrific condition a mile from where they had found his car. His body appeared to be a bag of trash at first. He was on his knees, bent over, with his face in the dirt. Twelve days of decomposition, the elements, and animal attacks made him virtually unrecognizable. Medical professionals used dental records to confirm that the body was indeed Doug Gissendaner. He had been stabbed four times in the head, neck, and back.

While there was a long list of potential suspects, investigators kept Kelly close. When they talked to her again to go over her initial statements, the pressure must have gotten to her. She finally admitted that she had spoken to Greg on occasion when he called her. She made it clear to police that she did not pursue any relationship with Greg, and he pursued her. She also admitted that she reconciled with Owen during a separation, and she told investigators that he said that he would kill Doug when he found that she was getting back together with him. At this time, she pointed the finger at Greg and police questioned him heavily. Their relationship was officially over.

With the investigation focused on Greg, Greg's roommate changed his story completely. He was afraid that his leis could get him in trouble, and he told the police a new story. In fact, he confessed to investigators that Greg had been gone the night before until 8 am the next morning. With Greg's alibi gone, investigators knew they were getting even closer to the truth.

Kelly's story was raveling apart as well when investigators pulled up phone records that showed 47 calls between the two. They also saw that Kelly initiated the calls 18 times, which goes against what she told them while interrogated that she only spoke to him because he constantly called her. Furthermore, the correspondence ended immediately after the murder. Why would they stop talking so suddenly for no reason? Her inconsistencies made her look bad to the investigators who were suspicious of her story from the beginning.

After more interrogation, Greg confessed to the murder after he was told that cooperation could prevent him from getting the death penalty. He proceeds to implicate Kelly to save himself. He explains how he and Kelly had an intimate relationship, and she told Greg that she wanted him to kill Doug after they settled into their new house. She even came up with alibis at this time. He goes on to describe the murder in detail. He stated that Kelly picked him up and allowed her into his house. She even gave him the nightstick and the knife that he would use to attack her husband. She advised him to make it look like a home invasion and robbery. Greg waited until Doug got home at around 11 pm, and then he forced him to drive out to the boondocks by knifepoint. They eventually stopped, and Greg forced Doug out of the car and told him to walk. He committed the horrible murder by hitting him in the head with the nightstick and then stabbing him repeatedly, leaving him to bleed. Once completed, Kelly arrived with kerosene to get rid of the evidence. After the murder, Kelly told Greg that they shouldn't speak anymore until things die down. This is the confession that Greg gave police. With this confession, Greg only received a sentence of twenty five years to life instead of the death penalty.

As soon as the police had Greg's confession, they went to also arrest Kelly. They barged into her home on February 25th and completed the arrest. Kelly changed her story once again after her arrest. She confessed that she saw Greg Owen the night of the murder. This time she said that he called her, and she went to pick him up. When he picked her up, he told her about the murder. He then proceeded to threated to murder her and her children as well if she did not help him. Even though the police didn't believe her, Kelly maintained her innocence. Greg was only lying to save himself! She even turned down the plea deal offered to her and decided to go to trial. It was the same plea deal that the prosecution gave Greg- a guilty plea would give her twenty five to life, but she would not get the death penalty. Even her lawyer suggested that she take the plea deal, but Kelly decided to go to trial.

**Trial**

The first day of Kelly's trial was on November 2, 1998. The jury consisted of two men and ten women. Reporters were prevalent throughout the proceedings.

Prosecutors started by painting a picture of a troubled marriage between Kelly and Doug and her affair with Greg Owen. They then claimed that Gissendaner killed her husband to receive the house he bought for the family and two $10,000 life insurance policies. The reward was surprisingly small but substantial enough to be considered a motive alongside her affair. Prosecution also pointed out inconsistencies in her police reports of the night and the fact that Kelly specifically waited until Doug had bought the house for her and her children. She even had the foresight to plan alibis. This indicated that the murder was premeditated.

The prosecution brought many people into court to testify against Kelly. She faced her late husband's father, who was a witness in her trial. He brought up the troubled marriage between Kelly and his murdered son as well as her questionable relationship with Greg. While many people tried to argue that Doug Sr. already disliked Kelly, his closeness to the situation proved effective.

Another witness was Laura McDuffie. Laura McDuffie was an inmate who was in jail with Kelly. While the defense pointed out that the convict may not be the most trustworthy source and McDuffie only wanted time off of her sentence, her claims were convincing. McDuffie confessed that Kelly offered her $10,000 to take the fall for the murder of Doug Gissendaner. Kelly went so far as to provide a map and a handwritten statement of what McDuffie should say. A handwriting expert confirmed that the statement was in fact written by Kelly.

Kelly's own friend Pam was a witness for the prosecution, too. Pam told the jury that Kelly called her and told her that she had killed Doug. She called back at a later time and said that Greg had forced her to do it by threatening to kill her and her children. Pam claimed that Kelly said, "I did it,", but the defense claimed that pam heard incorrectly. Other friends also stepped up to voice they're uneasiness with her behavior while her husband was missing.

The strongest witness for the prosecution, though, was Greg Owen. His statement matched very closely with his confession, but there were certain differences that poked holes in his statement. He originally said that he drove for some time and then Kelly arrived when Doug was dead. He changed the time that Kelly showed up to the murder scene as he was finishing murdering Doug. Doug originally stated that he and Kelly burned the car together, but he then changed his story to say that Kelly simply threw a bottle of kerosene out of the window for him and he burned the car alone. Even with some holes in his original story, the confession remained very damning for Kelly. The former lovers found themselves implicating each other in their once common scheme.

The defense stated that the prosecution could not prove Kelly's innocence beyond a reasonable doubt. Furthermore, Doug Gissendaner was significantly larger than Greg and was also trained by the military. It seemed unreasonable that Doug would obey Greg's commands even if he did have a knife. Greg showed no sign of injury or struggle. It also didn't seem fair that Greg only got a life sentence when he was the one who committed the murder. Also, Greg's testimony, which was part of a plea bargain, gave him incentive to implicate Kelly for a lower sentence for himself.

In the end, a trial of her peers found Kelly Gissendaner guilty after deliberating for only two hours and sentenced her to the death penalty. In just a couple of words, Kelly's life came to an end. However, she was going to do whatever she could to save herself.

**Life in Prison**

Kelly was taken to prison where she was the only woman on death row. Being on death row, Kelly did her best to retain a relationship with her three children. She also continued to appeal her case, focus on her spiritual health, and mentor other prisoners.

While on death row, Kelly could not socialize with the general prison population. However, she could preach and act as a spiritual guide by talking to inmates through a vent. Mrs. Gissendaner created a bit of a name for herself in prison, and the women inmates supported her throughout her trial. They even called themselves the Struggle Sisters and rallied for her to be taken off of death row and allowed to live the rest of her life in prison.

**Execution Reschedules**

Her actual execution was actually the third time that Gissendaner had been scheduled for execution. She was previously scheduled for execution at the end of February, but the date was changed due to complications with winter weather. Next, she was scheduled for execution in the first week of March, but the doctors at the prison were concerned because the drug used to perform the lethal injection appeared cloudy. They sent a specimen to be tested, and, in April, they announced the results that there was nothing wrong. Gissenander's lawyers tried claiming that the changes in her execution date constituted cruel and unusual treatment, but the case was thrown out. If anything, Kelly was given more time, but her lawyers fought to the end.

### Death

It was 12:21 a.m. on a Wednesday morning in Jackson, Georgia when officials declared Kelly MN Gissendaner dead from lethal injection. Her execution was scheduled for 7:00 p.m., but her lawyers attempted to repeal the decision to the very end. One hundred people stood outside of the Georgia Diagnostic and Classification Center in protest of her death. Her last meal was nachos, chips with cheese dip, and frozen lemonade.

Gissendaner showed remorse for her part in her ex-husband's death until the very end. Her last words were, "Bless you all. Tell the Gissendaners I am so, so sorry that an amazing man lost his life because of me. If I could take it all back, I would." Her words can be interpreted to indicate a sense of guilt on Gissendaner's part. It can also be interpreted to indicate a peace with her position.

Kelly Gissendaner was the only woman at death row for the entire duration of her time incarcerated, and she was the first woman to be given the death penalty in Georgia since 1945- over 70 years. She was one of only six women executed in the state, and she was the last woman to be executed in Georgia.

### Appeals and Support

Kelly's lawyers made a valiant attempt at an appeal. In fact, the appeal was more than fifty pages when they turned it in, and it had statements from a number of different people, including inmates, the pope, and political figures.

After being approached by Mrs. Gissendaner's lawyer, the pope responded in a letter stating, "While not wishing to minimize the gravity of the crime for which Ms. Gissendaner has been convicted, and while sympathizing with the victims, I nonetheless implore you, in consideration of the reasons that have been presented to your Board, to commute the sentence to one that would better express both justice and mercy."

The endorsement by the pope was powerful, but the Catholic Church had also just recently vocalized a stance against the death penalty. Even former Georgia Supreme Court Chief Justice Norman Fletcher stood up for the defendant saying that her role in the murder did not constitute the death penalty. In addition to these endorsements, 90,000 people also signed a petition to support Kelly. Kelly's lawyers showed the courts that Kelly showed remorse and represented a criminal who had turned her life around to bring positivity to those around her. They argued that her presence was significantly greater than her absence to those around her, especially her children and other inmates.

Mrs. Gissendaner's lawyers attempted three appeals to the U.S. Supreme Court, but they were denied all three times. Unfortunately, on the day of the execution, Mrs. Gissendaner's children had to choose between saying good-bye to their mother or appearing in front of a judge for one last attempt to appeal her case. The last time that they saw their mother was two days earlier on Monday. In the most heartbreaking of all testimonies, Kelly's daughter, Kayla pleaded with the court to save her mother's life. She made the point that she had already lost her dad, and he would not want her or her siblings to endure any further loss by also losing their mother. Despite the emotional appear and strong endorsements, the court did not waver on its original decision.

Despite the support from multiple sources, Douglas's family, especially his father, maintained throughout the trial that they trusted the legal system and agreed with the sentence of the death penalty. They reminded the public that she chose to go to trial instead of pleading guilty. They also reminded the public that Douglas did not get any choice in what happened to his life. After the gruesome death of their son, an exhausting and emotional search for the truth, and a prolonged trial, Douglas Gissendaner Sr. and Sue Gissendaner got justice.

### Death Penalty Debate

Kelly Gissendaner's case became famous across the nation because of its legal implications regarding the death penalty. People for the death penalty noted that Kelly had orchestrated the entire murder, she helped dispose of the body, she lied multiple times, and the family of Douglas Gissendaner deserved justice. People opposed to the death penalty noted that there was room for doubt, she technically did not commit the murder, the person who did commit the murder escaped the death penalty, she showed remorse over her part in the murder, she experienced trauma in her childhood, and she regularly preached and encouraged other women in the prison. Men and women all over the country debated the case, but, ultimately, the death penalty ruling was honored by the state of Georgia, and Kelly was executed while she sobbed and sang "Amazing Grace". She was 47-years-old.

# WENDI ANDRIANO

Chapter 1

A dying husband needs a devoted wife. But when love runs out, marriage becomes a burden.

On October 8, 2000, Wendi Andriano snapped. She had played the part of devoted wife to her terminally ill husband, Joe Andriano, for years, but when the love left their marriage, so did Wendi's patience for her husband's eventual demise.

Wendi had a plan to help nudge nature along, and when her plan b expired, she took matters directly into her own hands and bludgeoned him to death.

Wendi first tried to poison her husband by spiking his last meal, a homemade beef stew, with sodium azide, but Joe Andriano did not ingest enough to kill him, only enough to vomit it back up. Wendi then grabbed the nearest object, a bar stool, and beat her dying husband over the head so many times that parts of his brain became exposed.

After thinking she had successfully killed her husband twice, Wendi then realized that Joe was still breathing, so she took a knife from the family kitchen and stabbed him in the side of the throat.

Minutes later, Joe was finally dead.

This bizarre and frantic way Wendi killed her husband isn't the strangest thing about the case though. Known even to Wendi, Joe was due to die from terminal cancer within the next few years anyways.

Why Wendi couldn't wait to kill her husband is an intriguing tale wrought with sex, lies, and strangely, a lack of patience.

Chapter 2

Wendi and Joe Andriano grew up together in the small farming community of Casa Grande, Arizona. But while they both had gone to the same school, they never dated. As a minister's daughter, Wendi's social life was restricted to her father's church. Her celebration for graduating high school was even in the form of a missionary trip to

Mexico in 1989. When she returned she took a job at the local clerical hospital.

Wendi met Joe in 1992 through friends. Although when the couple started dating Joe's family found the minister's daughter to be an unusual fit for the loud, outgoing former football player, they all thought she was friendly enough and approved of the match.

Joe worked for a local boat builder. He was very mechanically inclined and was a very good welder. He owned his own boat and took Wendi for several cruises around the local hot spots for speedboats. They were inseparable.

The couple married in January of 1994. Their wedding took place in a baptist church across the street from their shared elementary school. Their reception was at the Elk's club and was populated by their many friends and family. Even after two years of dating, though, Joe's family felt like they didn't know his new bride very well, but Joe seemed to be very happy, so they were happy for him.

Soon after marrying, the couple became business partners when they started a small company that did windshield repair and replacement. The business combined Wendi's office experience with Joe's mechanical experience, skills they both exceeded at, and the business thrived.

The couple hadn't been married a whole year yet before they faced their first major challenge together. That fall, Joe noticed an odd bump on his neck. When he had it tested, he was told it was a non-cancerous benign tumor, but it wasn't long before they were second-guessing the diagnoses. A year after it was removed, the tumor grew back.

A second surgery and round of tests seemed to reconfirm that the tumor was benign, but shortly after Wendi gave birth to a son in 1997, the tumor was back yet again.

The third time the tumor returned, Joe's wife and family were convinced that the tumor had to be cancer. This fear was confirmed in 1998 when Joe underwent surgery to have the bump removed for the fourth time. Joe's pre-surgery chest x-ray showed that not only was the tumor cancerous, but that the cancer had now spread across Joe's throat, chest, and lungs.

The prognosis wasn't good—Joe had a rare form of cancer and while radiation and chemotherapy were standard, there was no guarantee they would work. On top of this, Wendi was also pregnant again and was only months away from giving birth to the couple's second child.

Chapter 3

In an effort to increase Joe's chances of survival while decreasing his suffering, Wendi and Joe decided to pursue holistic treatments before resorting to chemotherapy and radiation. They had been told that chemotherapy and radiation treatments would likely not cure Joe, but they would lengthen his life by a few years; however, these years would be anything from pleasant. The horrific side-effects chemotherapy and radiation treatments cause are well known.

So the Andriano's decided first to try anything from special diets to alternative medical treatments to prayer—anything that had a chance to help Joe. Joe even attended a holistic treatment centre for cancer patients in Colorado for a few weeks where he was surrounded by other men and women facing the same prognosis as him. After seeing the bravery of others in the same position as him, Joe began thinking about his future again and began to see it as bright for the first time in a while.

After Joe returned from his holistic healing getaway with a bright new attitude, the Andriano's decided the next best step would be for Joe to begin chemotherapy treatments. He had begun to crave his future and was ready to take steps to achieve it. Unfortunately, taking these steps meant that Joe needed to quit his welding job as well as his own position in the couple's business.

To help make ends meet, Wendi returned to working for the first time since the birth of the couple's children. She ended up taking multiple jobs and worked long hours while continuing to care for her husband at home. Eventually, Wendi landed a job managing the San Riva apartment complex in the Ahwatukee foothills, an upscale neighbourhood outside of Phoenix.

Wendi's new job came with some major perks—the salary was above average, which was nice as Wendi was now the family's breadwinner, and it required Wendi to live on site, which meant that the family now lived in a luxury apartment but paid no rent. Wendi's new job also gave her a new life. A large part of her duties as complex manager was arranging social activities for the other residents of the San Riva apartments, who were mostly young, wealthy, single businesspeople.

Every Saturday the complex hosted picnics, pool parties, or late-night socials. The residents even had their own baseball team. Wendi was required to attend every event, which meant Joe was needed to stay home with their two children. Wendi enjoyed this alone time so much that many of the residents at the San Riva had no clue she had a dying husband and two children at home. She partied like she was single.

The first few months at the San Riva went well. Wendi organized mixers and pool parties for the tenants while Joe took care of the kids. Despite being very weak from treatments, he did everything he could, he wanted to do it. He preferred to have his kids around him even when he didn't feel good.

Although they had never gotten close to their daughter-in-law, Joe's parents also pitched in with babysitting so the couple could have time alone together. They didn't get to see each other much as Wendi began spending more and more time at work. Her new job had also given her a new confidence, and she spent many nights out on the town dancing and drinking away her weekday stress with friends. Joe began to fear that Wendi would soon leave him for her new lifestyle, but this fear got sidetracked when his health continued to fail.

In the summer of 2000, when tests revealed his cancer had spread yet again, Joe and Wendi decided to increase the frequency of Joe's chemotherapy. Joe agreed to undergo more treatments, but they quickly took their toll. He lost 15 pounds in the first week alone, and Joe's doctor became concerned. It went from bad to worse very quickly.

By the beginning of October 2000, it became harder and harder to remain optimistic about Joe's chances of beating his cancer. It became apparent it was terminal, but doctors insisted that with treatment Joe could live for several more years.

No one had any idea that Joe would be dead after only the first week of the month. No one, that is, except for one person—Wendi Andriano.

Chapter 4

Just after 2:00 a.m. on October 8, Wendi Andriano called a friend who also lived in the San Riva apartment complex. She told her friend that she needed someone to stay with the kids while she took Joe to the hospital. When the friend arrived, she found Joe on the floor, barely alive.

Joe was on the floor in the fetal position. There was vomit on the floor around him and he couldn't stand up. Wendi confided in her friend that she told Joe that she had called 9-1-1 and paramedics were on the way, but this wasn't true. After seeing Joe in such poor condition, the neighbour urged Wendi to call paramedics. She then went outside to wait for them to arrive while Wendi waiting with her husband.

Wendi did call 9-1-1, but when the EMT's arrived minutes later, she refused to let them or her friend inside the apartment. She said that her husband was dying from terminal cancer and had a do not resuscitate order. Joe was not to receive any medical attention.

Just over an hour later, at 3:30 a.m., Wendi dialed 9-1-1 a second time. The same team of paramedics came to the house. It didn't take them long to realize something wasn't quite right, so they contacted the police department. Both the paramedics and the police were shocked to find out that Joe, who had been terminally ill from cancer for quite some time had died, but not from the cancer that had been slowly killing his body. He died from being repeatedly beaten with a bar stool and from being stabbed in the neck.

When the police opened the front door of the apartment, they were confronted with obvious signs of a deadly struggle. The apartment was in a complete state of disarray, and there was blood everywhere. Blood had been traced throughout the kitchen, the dining room, and the living room of the luxury apartment, and blood had spattered across the walls the ceilings. Lying in the middle of the bloody scene was Joe, with a knife wound in his neck and holes spattered across his visible skull.

While crime scene technicians surveyed the apartment, phoenix police took Wendi down to the station for a formal statement. She was wearing clothes drenched in Joe's blood and was armed with a story that explained how Joe's death had been a complete accident.

In the interrogation room, Wendi told police she and joe had spent the evening in Casa Grande visiting with Joe's parents. They put the kids to bed after they returned home, which was when Joe noticed something odd about Wendi's appearance—she wasn't wearing her wedding ring.

According to Wendi, Joe worked himself into a rage and began accusing her of having an affair. This argument turned into a shoving match, and when Joe grabbed a belt, Wendi grabbed a bar stool and swung. Joe went down on all fours so she hit him again. It was then that she called her neighbour for help. Joe may have been in a terrible state when the neighbour saw him, but according to Wendi when she went outside Joe had gotten back to his feet easily.

Wendi said she denied the EMTs access to the apartment because she and Joe were both embarrassed about the fight, but just minutes after the EMTs left, the fight got physical again.

Wendi said that her husband tried to strangle her with a telephone cord and she defended herself with the first weapon she could get in her hands—a kitchen knife. She was vague about how the knife ended up in Joe's neck though, saying she was holding the knife up when Joe suddenly fell flat on his face. The next thing she knew, blood was spurting everywhere. He must have fallen on the blade, it was simply an accident.

Many things about this story didn't make sense to the police. First of all, the timeline presented in Wendi's story didn't match the accounts of Wendi's neighbour or the EMTs. Wendi's neighbour had seen no evidence of a physical fight when they first entered the apartment—there were no broken bar stools or blood like later when the police arrived. As well, Wendi had few injuries on her body, definitely no injuries that would necessitate self defence in the form of murder.

Joe's illness also shed doubt on Wendi's story. Joe's parents told police that when the Andriano's visited earlier that evening, Joe had been so weak from his treatments that he could barely stand. They had spent the evening doting on their sick son, bringing him any comforts he wanted. If he was too weak to stand, he certainly couldn't have been strong enough to violently attack Wendi.

Police also uncovered a damning piece of evidence from Wendi herself, in a moment when she thought she was all alone. The investigators that had been questioning Wendi left her on her own in the interrogation room for some time while they fact checked some of her statements and checked in with the investigators who were scanning the crime scene for evidence. During this time, Wendi made a phone call to a coworker at the apartment complex and asked them to hide some of her files from the police. This immediately led to a search of Wendi's office where police found evidence that Wendi had in fact killed her husband. She had even been planning it for months.

Chapter 5

While both investigators strongly believed that Wendi Andriano was responsible for Joe's death, they were stumped by her motive. Why would Wendi kill her dying husband? The police didn't know, but they did have one intriguing lead—the phone call Wendi had made from the interrogation room. They were determined to find out what she was trying to hide.

When they searched her office, police discovered that Wendi had been disciplined at work for using her computer to search inappropriate items on the internet while on the clock.She had been conducting research on poisons, and how to use certain poisons to kill people. They also discovered the papers that she had tried to hide—shipping notices for a substance known as sodium azide.

Sodium azide is a lethal substance with a variety of industrial uses including propelling airbags. It is not, however, something that the average person can simply go out and buy. It's not restricted to the point where only certain companies can possess it, but it needs to be bought for a reason—something that an apartment complex didn't have. But based on the information on the shipping invoice, Wendi had found a way around that.

Wendi had created a fictitious business license using the tax ID form for the apartment complex. Using a Xerox machine and an exacto knife, Wendi had removed all information specific to the apartment complex and inserted fictitious information for a fake company.

The business name on the shipping notice was bogus, but the address wasn't. Wendi had the substance delivered to an address in Scottsdale, Arizona in an attempt to distance herself, but that plan didn't work. When the police tracked down the real address on the invoice, workers at the company positively identified Wendi as the person who had come by a couple weeks earlier to pick up a package she had mistakenly had shipped there instead of her own office.

Wendi's coworkers had seen her with a package but that she had been very mysterious with the contents. She refused to tell anyone what was inside. Had this been the sodium azide? And if so, where was it now?

Chapter 6

Suspecting that Wendi had tried to poison Joe with the sodium azide, police took samples of every medication and food they could find in the Andriano's apartment. If Joe had ingested poison, it would have explained the awful state Wendi's friend had seen him in just over an hour before he died. Luckily, the remainders of Joe's last supper, homemade beef stew, still sat in a pot on the stove.

However, police didn't find any evidence of Wendi's mysterious package, or any evidence of the sodium azide itself in Wendi and Joe's apartment. They had just begun to lose hope in finding the poison when they found out Wendi had a storage space in the building that she failed to tell the police about. Hidden behind a stack of boxes in Wendi's storage unit was a small bottle of white powder and a measuring spoon. The white powder was soon identified as sodium azide.

But the storage unit wasn't the only place investigators found the lethal substance—it was also in Joe's stomach contents and in the beef stew on the stove.

While discovering the poison helped police understand that Wendi had been trying to kill her husband, it didn't explain why she had bludgeoned him to death on October 8, 2000. Wendi had spent a lot of time researching poisons and she spent a lot of time manufacturing documents so that she could purchase the poison. It certainly wasn't a spur of the moment decision.

But why would Wendi beat and stab her husband if she had already poisoned him? Prosecutors had a theory, one that would cut to the heart of the crime. It was patience—or more precisely, Wendi's lack of it—that had killed Joe in the end.

Wendi had grown tired of waiting for the cancer to kill Joe, so she decided to give nature a little nudge by poisoning his supper. But according to the theory, when Wendi gave Joe the poison, things didn't go quite to plan. Joe hadn't ingested enough poison to kill him when he began vomiting it back up. With her plan quickly failing, Wendi panicked. She snapped.

Now improvising, Wendi beat Joe with the nearest object she could get her hands on—a bar stool. Pathologists were able to conclude that Wendi beat Joe over the head with the stool no less than twenty-four times. This beating did render Joe unconscious, but still didn't kill him so Wendi grabbed a kitchen knife and stabbed him in the part of his body that caused all this trouble in the first place—the side of his neck.

Chapter 7

Ten days after she murdered her husband, Wendi Andriano was formally charged with first degree murder. Wendi's crime was viewed as being especially cruel due to the large amount of suffering Joe had had to endure over several hours thanks to Wendi's actions. Because of this, the prosecutor's on Wendi's trial did the almost unthinkable, they sought the death penalty.

When Wendi a walked into the Arizona courtroom on September 9, 2004 she looked vastly different from the perky apartment manager that the residents of the San Riva apartments used to know.

At the time of the killing she had been blonde, she had short hair, and generally appeared to be much younger and cute than the individual who appeared in court with long dark hair and thick glasses. Previously, she had liked to look good and show her figure so her conservative dress at the trial was certainly different from the look her friends were used to seeing. She was trying to look more conservative, more innocent.

She had had plenty of time to perfect her new look—it had taken prosecutors almost four years to bring the case to trial. It had been postponed about 12 times before it was finally brought before a judge and jury.

In their opening statement, prosecutors reminded the jury that at the time of the murder Wendi had been anything but the perfect mother or wife she claimed to have been. She had been someone who had no disregard for her husband at all. While her husband was dying, she had gone out partying and started affairs, and when his condition worsened, and it began to cramp her style, she turned to poison.

Wendi didn't like her new role as family breadwinner, especially with the loss of Joe's income, and with rising medical bills, the family was in the worst financial state they had ever been in. Wendi had thought she was going to be able to be a stay-at-home-mom for the rest of her life, and she did not adjust well to her return to the workforce. So Wendi had found an out.

Although Joe did not have any life insurance, even though Wendi had asked several friends to pretend to be Joe in medical exams so he could be insured, Joe had filed a malpractice suit against his former doctor who had continually told him his tumor was benign when it was in fact spreading throughout his body. If Joe died and the lawsuit went through, Wendi would likely walk away with a multi-million dollar settlement.

More than money though, Wendi had wanted freedom. She wanted the freedom to be single again, she wanted freedom to the ball-and-chain who was slowly dragging her spirit into his grave along with himself. Wendi wanted to not have to care about her dying husband anymore, who was too weak to provide her with any love.

Wendi maintained her plea of innocence throughout the trial, and her defence team attempted to prove she had been the victim of abuse not only on the night of Joe's death but also throughout the couple's entire marriage. To explain the poison, Wendi told the court that Joe had been the one who had grown tired of waiting for the cancer to end his life, and had asked Wendi to help him do it himself.

On the witness stand Wendi said that Joe had willingly taken the poison, but she also stuck by the story that she had originally told police, that Joe had suspected an affair and became enraged when she affirmed them. He became deranged and attacked her, starting the bloody fight. Wendi claimed Joe had died during the ensuing struggle.

Wendi's story wasn't enough to convince the court though, and on November 18, 2004 she was found guilty of the crime. It had taken the jury only two-and-a-half-hours to come to its unanimous decision. Six years after her husband joe had been diagnosed with terminal cancer, Wendi Andriano faced a possible death sentence of her own.

On December 20, 2004, the jurors assigned to Wendi Andriano's case met and decided on Wendi's fate—it would be death for Ms Andriano. Wendi, along with most of the courtroom, was aghast. Even Joe's family was shocked by the decision. Wendi Andriano became the second ever woman to be put on death row in Arizona, a state that reserves the death penalty for the worst of the worst.

Wendi Andriano has since attempted to appeal the court's decision, but as of early 2017, all attempts have been denied and Wendi continues to wait on death row. Wendi and Joe's children now live with Joe's parents, who continue to mourn the loss of their beloved son.

Joe Andriano's death was especially long, and especially cruel, but no happy ending was found when Wendi was sentenced to her own death. Many view the conclusion of this case to be the saddest possible outcome. On October 8, 2000, two lives were lost, and two children were left without parents.

# HUSBAND KILLER : THE TRUE STORY OF LARISSA SCHUSTER

67

## ERIN EDWARDS

Larissa Leann Foreman was born January 1, 1960. She grew up on a farm near Clarence Missouri. By all accounts she had a happy childhood. She won first place at the Randolph pony show, her father, Charles, won first place in the men's division and Deeann, her mom, won second in the bareback for pleasure division. Her parents seemed to be very involved in her life. She excelled academically; she was athletic and went after what she wanted with everything she had. She was described as a 'go getter'.

Larissa graduated High school and went on to the University of Missouri Columbia to become a biochemist. She didn't come from a rich family so she would work as a nursing aide at Boone Hospital Center in Columbia Missouri. It's not known whether she liked her work as an aide, however she did like a nurse named Tim Schuster, and he liked her as well. She was electrifying and intoxicating, Tim was enthralled. They started dating after becoming friends and just hanging out together after work.

Finally, in 1982 Tim popped the question, and Larissa said yes. Between 1982 and the birth of their second child Tyler in 1990 there was a whirlwind of things happening. There was the wedding in '82, the birth of their first child, Kristin, and a move to sunny central California, Fresno to be exact.

In the beginning Tim managed the cardiology Department for St Agnes Medical Center. While Larissa worked for Pan Agricultural Laboratories. Larissa saw the company declining and thought it a good time to start her own company; Central California Research Lab. She was ambitious and worked long hours to make her company a success. Tim continued to work at St Agnes and be both Mom and Dad to their two children.

According to friends Bob and Mary Solis, Tim was the one who made sure doctor appointments were kept, homework was done and dinner was cooked and on the table. Larissa ruled her house and Tim having a non-confrontational personality went along with her, if for no other reason than to keep the peace. By this time she was making more than twice what Tim made. It was her money that made it possible for them to move to Clovis and buy a much larger home than the one they had in Fresno. It looked like they had it all...but did they?

By this time Kristen was a teenager and as with most teens there was attitude. Kristen fought with her mother at almost every turn. She stood up to Larissa in such a way that she felt she had no other option than to send her daughter to her parents in Clarence, Missouri. Tim was upset that his wife didn't even discuss this move with him; she'd decided this IS what will happen. And soon his beloved little girl was gone. But still Tim kept quiet.

The Schuster's entered into a bitter, rancorous separation in 2002, after nearly 20 years of marriage and two children. They tried living in the same house after the separation. However Larissa was not happy with this arrangement. From the very beginning she didn't want Tim to have anything to do with Tyler, no visitation and no kind of a relationship with his son at all. This was not okay with Tim. On more than one occasion she made the statement that she wished Tim would just die.

In late June or early July Larissa took Tyler and went on a trip out of state. Tim took this opportunity to secure a condo and move out of the family's home. Larissa was livid that he would have the nerve to leave while she was away and accused him of taking things from the house that didn't belong to him. What earlier seemed like idle threats became something more, she told a neighbor that she should just get it over with and kill Tim herself.

A Plan started formulating shortly after Tim moved out of the Clovis family home. Larissa asked James Fagone a lab assistant and Larissa's sometimes babysitter, sometimes whipping boy if he would help break in to Tim's house and help her get back somethings he took when he moved out. She felt he wasn't entitled to them and left messages on his answering machine telling him he'd better bring them back...or else.

After returning from a trip Tim came home to a house that had been burglarized and ransacked. One of the things missing...the very set of mixing bowls Larissa had had such a fit over. Who was her accomplice in the break-in...none other than James Fagone? Larissa wasn't shy about what they had done, she told her manicurist Terri Lopez, that after the break-in she would go back to Tim's house and sit in a chair and look around at what they had done. She also told Tami Belshay that "it gave her a feeling that was better than sex."

After the burglary the Schuster's relationship went even further downhill. Tim knew who had broken into his condo. Larissa's bitterness not only let her destroy things in the condo, but she even bragged about keying his truck. She said it made her happy every time she saw the marks on his truck. Tim seemed worried about what his estranged wife was capable of. He moved again, this time to a house in Clovis that had motion sensors and an alarm. He obtained a handgun and a permit to carry a concealed weapon. Larissa had told her manicurist Ms. Lopez that she prayed every night that Tim would just die. At one point Larissa told her that she could kill Tim and get away with it. She also asked one of the employees at CCRL if her boyfriend knew anyone that would kill Tim or at least rough him up. She'd made remarks like this before and all who heard them thought she was just venting because the divorce wasn't going the way she wanted it to. She said she would do anything to keep Tim from getting the business.

According to Bob and Mary Solis, Larissa would belittle and embarrass Tim in front friends and family alike. She seemed to relish the power she had over him.

In late June St Agnes let everyone know that there would be a round of layoffs coming and to be expecting it. Tim and his friend Mary Solis was on the short list to be let go. Larissa laughed when she heard the news. On July 9th Tim, Mary, her husband Bob and another friend Victor Uribe all had dinner together. The group broke up about 10pm that night, before Tim left the Solis' they had made arrangements to meet for breakfast the next morning. Tim never showed for his exit meeting or for breakfast. This worried Bob and Mary, it seems Tim was never late for anything, and if he thought he was going to be late he called. He was also supposed to pick up Tyler that evening.

His friends tried to reach Tim, calling his cell phone. Finally they called Uribe and told him that they couldn't reach Tim and would he go by the house and check on their friend. Uribe arrived at Tim's house and went inside. There didn't seem to be anything out of place, until he went to the bedroom. Tim's watch, wallet and cell phone were lying on the dresser. Uribe was now worried as well. Victor said "He never went anywhere without his cell, he kept it with him at all times, in case the kids needed him."

No one knew what had happened to Tim. The police refused to even take a missing person's report until he'd been missing 24 hours. July 10th when Tim had not been heard from in the allotted time Bob Solis filed the missing person's report. Officer John Willow from the Clovis Police Department responded to the call.

Willow found Tim's handgun under a cushion of a chair. He found Tim's cell phone in the bedroom and called all the numbers in his contacts to see if any of them had seen or heard from Mr. Schuster. When he called Larissa she said she hadn't heard from him either. He also talked to Terri Lopez and she relayed to Willow that the Schuster's were going through a rather nasty divorce. John Willow decided to turn the case over to Detectives Larry Kirkhart and Vincent Weibert.

When they entered Tim's home they noted some damage on the wall behind the chair where the gun was found earlier. They found a briefcase in the same room as the chair. Inside they found a microcassette recorder and tape. In the bedroom they found an answering machine that showed only one number, a cell phone number belonging to Larissa Schuster. Detective Kirkhart then asked Larissa to come to the police station for a chat about her missing husband.

During her interview with the detectives she told them that she and Tim were getting a divorce and that they did not communicate very well with each other. They asked her about her cell number being on the caller ID. She fabricated a story about being asleep on her couch and waking up to find she had pushed some buttons and maybe she had speed dialed Tim. They asked her if she had her phone with her and she said no. Kirkhart called for a pause in the interview and went to the parking lot to find Larissa's car. He looked in the window and saw a phone on the center console, dialed her number and the phone in the car rang.

Kirkhart went back to the interview room and asked Larissa to come with them to unlock her car and retrieve her phone. Back inside the station the interview resumed. The detective went through her contacts that she had on speed dial, none of them were Tim's number.

Larissa's whole demeanor changed, she was shaking and in the opinion of the detectives showing signs of deceit. She came clean and admitted that she had lied to the detectives and she knew she shouldn't have. She claimed she wasn't trying to be deceitful. None the less they let Schuster go home, for now. At this point in their investigation they still had no idea what had happened to Tim. Kirkhart had asked Larissa if she thought that Tim could just cash out some money and leave town, go camping or to Vegas to just get away. She told them she didn't think he would do that, that he wouldn't leave his son like that. This was still just a missing person case and most of Tim's friends thought that perhaps he had just had enough, the divorce, the custody battle, losing his job was to much for him to handle. Tami Belshay, Bob and Mary Solis and Victor Uribe were among those friends. The detectives were thinking the same thing at this point.

With no solid leads on Tim's whereabouts detectives Weibert and Kirkhart kept searching for some clue, however small that might give them some direction on finding Tim. Kirkhart was going through Tim's ledger provided to them by Larissa. And they came across a name they were familiar with...James Fagone. They knew his name because he was the one suspected of breaking into Tim's house with Larissa shortly after Tim moved out of the family home a year earlier. They also knew that he was an associate of sorts of Larissa's.

The following Monday Detectives Kirkhart and Daly called Fagone to come and talk with them. Vince Weibert thought that perhaps Fagone might have some "inside" information on Tim's disappearance.

It seems that Fagone was a babysitter for the Schuster's son Tyler, before and after their separation. James was a good kid according to his attorney Peter Jones. "He's an above average student, higher than a 4.0 grade point average...a gentle spirit."

Fagone was nervous during the police interview. He admitted that Larissa had him help her break into Tim's house and take back things that she didn't want him to have.

James told the detectives that Larissa was going around the house looking for things and he just wanted to get the TV and some other stuff so he wasn't paying attention to what she was doing. Obviously James was scared out of his mind by now, but they pressed him more telling him they "knew he was involved somehow" with Tim's disappearance. Fagone's determination not to tell what had happened, what him and Larissa Schuster had done crumbled.

Fagone confessed that he had been there the night that Tim went missing, that he had gone to his house with a weapon. James relayed to them that Larissa had paid him the $2000 to purchase a stun gun and that he could just keep the rest for himself.

So as the day wore on James conveyed the sordid details of the night in questions.

On the night that Tim lost his job at St Agnes and had dinner with a group of friends, James had done what he was told to do by

Larissa, buy a stun gun. Later he would get the call from her (Larissa). She picked him up and went to Tim's house. James laid in wait in the darkness just outside of his door. He could hear Larissa on the phone telling Tim that Tyler wasn't feeling well and she needed him to come to the front door.

A few moments later Tim opened the front door and James sprung from the shadows and attacked him wrestling him to the ground. Tim was struggling; James was using the stun gun on him, on the arm at first, not sure where else he might have zapped him. Soon Tim stopped struggling and when James looked up he saw Larissa with a rag that had been soaked in chloroform.

Were the detectives hearing this right? Was Fagone confessing to the murder of Timothy Schuster? But if they were going to believe any of it they needed some kind of evidence. They asked about the stun gun again, and what had Fagone done with it. He told them he threw it in a portable toilet on the edge of town. The investigators found the stun gun, right where James told them it should be.

Now at the same time Fagone was being interviewed Clovis Police Department got a call from a woman saying that her boss ask her to do something that in retrospect seemed a little off, suspicious even. Her Boss...Larissa Schuster. Leslie Dodd had been instructed to rent a moving truck by her boss. She was told to use her personal credit card and rent it in her own name not her boss's. A year earlier Larissa had asked the same employee to rent a storage unit near Schuster's lab, again to do it in the employees name and with her personal credit card.

Jim Koch got the call to check it out. He went to the storage unit and walked down the hall. He had been told to look for a blue barrel. When he found Schuster's unit and opened the door "there was a very very strong odor." Koch said. "I had on a breathing apparatus and gloves."

He saw the blue barrel, he opened it.

Koch said in an interview, "And when I opened the barrel I—I saw something that was very, very shocking to me and I recognized immediately as human remains. There was a barrel that's over 3/4 of the way full of fluid and portions of—of—body protruding from the fluid. And the body was obviously decaying. It was placed in acid. And the acid was basically eating away at the body."

Had Larissa Schuster killed her husband and put him in the barrel? According to James Fagone, yes she had, and he had helped her and then watched as she poured a caustic solution in on top of Tim. Worst of all, Tim was probably still alive when the acid was poured on him and he was sealed inside the barrel.

Tim had been found, the truth had come out and the Clovis detectives were on their way to Missouri to arrest Larissa for the murder of her husband Tim. They met her at the airport where she had gone to see her family. According to the detectives that arrested her for the murder she didn't even ask what had happened to Tim or how he died.

Both James Fagone and Larissa Schuster were arrested and charged with 1st degree murder.

Now that the perpetrators of Tim Schuster's murder had been arrested it was time to take them to trial. The murder was committed in the early morning hours of July 10, 2003. There was a lot left to do before the trial could begin.

The Clovis police department had to finish gathering evidence, talk to friends and family to make sure that everything was done correctly. They wanted to make sure that Larissa and James would not be let go on a technicality.

The judge had to decide if he would make this a death penalty case or a life in prison without parole case. That would be decided later. The prosecutor had to prepare a rock solid case and present the evidence to a jury in a manner that would guarantee a conviction. The defense would also be talking to people on behalf of their clients. Find people that had nothing but good things to say about them in hopes of offsetting the horrible truths that would come out at trial.

The judge separated the cases and James and Larissa would be tried separately. James was tried first. His attorney portrayed James as a misguided man who hero worshipped Larissa.

He was found guilty and is now serving a life without parole sentence.

There was so much media coverage on Larissa that the defense asked and received a change of venue. Her trial was moved to Los Angeles.

Monday October 22, 2007 Larissa's trial started. Prosecutor Dennis Peterson relayed to the jury of 9 women and 3 men just how the murder went down. He told them that Tim was still alive when the acid was poured over him while he laid head first inside the blue barrel. Her motive? She didn't want to share anything that they built during their 19 ½ years of marriage. She felt Tim didn't deserve any part of the business, or home and didn't want him to have contact with their tween son, Tyler.

CCRL employees would also testify to the facts of the blue barrel being at the lab and the day Tim was reported missing went to look for it and it was gone. They also said that Larissa had said that she should just shove Tim in the barrel and get rid of him.

A large amount of Hydrochloric acid, 12 gallons and Sulfuric acid, 4 gallons was ordered for Schuster's lab, more than ever before. Leslie Dodd (nee Fichera) testified that, "that was more acid than the lab would use in a year."

Joseph Boatwright thought Larissa was joking when she asked "if he thought a body would fit in the blue barrel."

Juror's watched several hours of Larissa's police interview. She made Tim out to be controlling and having a volatile temper. After seeing that part of the interview Bob Solis testified to the contrary, that Tim was very calm and a non-violent, non-confrontational person.

In another part of the interview with Clovis Detectives Schuster stated that "she prayed that Tim would get over this hostility about the divorce." Her manicurist Terri Lopez told a different story. Lopez said that "she told me she prayed every night he would die."

A hair stylist Becky Holland sometimes did Larissa's hair. During those appointments Larissa would rant about Tim. Holland didn't think much about it because she knew they were going through a divorce. Later though she said the hateful remarks escalated, Holland told the court, "this is getting a little creepy. It was so intense."

The jurors got to hear just how intense it was when they got to hear message after message of Larissa calling her husband awful names and making threats about their children. The prosecutor used these recordings to make a point to the jury; Larissa was in a "murderous rage". Nuttall interjected that these messages were left on Tim's machine 7 months before the murder.

And with this the prosecution rested, hoping that they had proved their case. There was one witness that they really needed to be able to lockdown the case against Schuster, they needed James Fagone. The judge had barred his confession so the jury would never hear in his own words what happened July 10, 2003. But he refused to cooperate with Peterson because he had already filed his appeal. The only thing that might have helped Peterson is the fact that James Fagone had already been convicted of Tim's murder.

Nuttall began the defense's case by telling the jury that neither he nor his client could tell them what had happened to Tim because "we don't know". And since the jury heard nearly nothing about Fagone, Roger Nuttall blamed the murder on him. After all Fagone had already been found guilty of the murder Larissa was now on trial for. Nuttall said in his opening statements that "Tim was an angry man who belittled Larissa in over-compensation for his own failings as a husband and father." And that "he began stalking Larissa after the divorce proceedings started."

Now Defense attorney Nuttall brought in a stream of witnesses that would steer the blame away from his client.

He had a medical expert that said the victim's body was cut in half and that the police had completely missed a second crime scene and the evidence from there would have proved that Fagone and others were responsible for Tim's murder not Larissa.

Nuttall even had psychiatrist Stephen Estner on the stand. Estner said that, "My impression was that Mrs. Schuster was a very direct and assertive person, and Mr. Schuster was a more passive and nurturing personality. And I think they started butting heads over that."

Larissa Schuster took the stand in her own defense and adamantly denied the charges saying, "No, I did not kill my husband." Again James Fagone would have the whole murder put squarely on him. Schuster told the jury, ""I heard him say something like 'there had been an accident and Tim is dead.' I thought he was joking."

She said that the $2000 payment to Fagone was for babysitting Tyler and housesitting while she was away on vacation with her son. Schuster said the large amount of acid was for cleaning a large scale of lab glass. Schuster seemed to explain everything away poking holes in the prosecutor's case. Would it be enough to get an acquittal? Had she actually swayed the jury?

It seemed that the trial was plagued with problems, including accusations of juror misconduct. At least one juror was replaced by an alternate due to disruptive behavior. Another admonished for giving Larissa a 'thumbs up' after her testimony. And yet with all of that...it was time for the jury to deliberate of the weeks of testimony they'd heard.

It took a little more than two days for the jury to decide on a verdict.

Guilty of Murder with a special circumstance of financial gain. The verdict came exactly one year after Fagone's.

Roger Nuttall slowed the sentencing of Larissa Schuster while he tried to find reasons to ask for a new trial. He even used the argument that there may have been juror misconduct. Nuttall wanted to talk to the jurors but Ellison said no. Nuttall appealed and the District court of Appeals told Ellison to contact the jurors on Schuster's behalf. All the jurors and alternates refused to speak to her attorney.

So on May 8, 2008, five months after being found guilty of her estranged husband's murder Larissa Leeann Schuster was sentenced to life in prison without the possibility of parole. Judge Ellison also denied her request for a new trial.

At the sentencing a total of seven people stood up to make statements about how they had been affected by the murder of Timothy Allen Schuster.

Kristen, Tim and Larissa's oldest child and only daughter made an emotionally charged statement to and about her mother.

She called her mother a demon for "taking my father away." And told her. "I pray you're continually haunted at night by the sight and sound of my father fighting for his last breathing moments on this earth. I hope you toss and turn and have horrible nightmares visualizing the horrific act of violence you have committed. Maybe later in life I can learn to forgive you, but I doubt it. This is goodbye, not just for now, but forever. This is goodbye as your daughter."

Kristen was so devastated over her father's murder she reached out to a support group murdervictims.com. Several people shared their own experiences of losing a parent at a young age hoping she could find at least a little peace.

# ALICIA SHAYNE LOVERA

The life of Alicia Shayne Lovera looked like something out of a soap opera.

Born into poverty, she was ushered into a life of wealth and privilege when her mother married a rich president of a bank. She grew up to be beautiful, popular and spoiled. But she soon find herself in financial ruin when her stepfather committed suicide, leaving the family with nothing.

Her sense of entitlement still intact, she married a struggling math teacher who couldn't resist her charms.

But when the marriage became an inconvenience, she did what all black widows do.

She killed her husband.

This is her story.

EARLY LIFE

Alicia Shayne Good was born in 1966 to teenage parents. Going by her middle name Shayne, her early life wasn't easy as her parents lacked the necessary resources to provide. Her mother would divorce her father. But when Shayne turned seven-years old things to a turn for the better.

"Her mother and she were poor," journalist Jamie Satterfield said. "Her mother met Brent Mills who was a bank president and they married into that family and Brent adopted Shayne."

The change in life circumstance was jarring to the young Shayne. She was instantly given an upgrade in lifestyle as she the world was now her oyster. There were expensive vacations, cars and garish parties.

Her new stepfather, Brent Mills, was a bank executive who treated Alicia and her mother Sandy to all the spoils his job could bring. He was well regarded in the business community and had several contacts.

But Brent had inherited the bank built by his father and lacked his business acumen. He was lenient in granting loans and the bank soon grew insolvent. He was also suspected of using the bank as a money laundering service for drug dealers.

On the surface, Brent told the family that the allegations were all fraudulent. He gave them every assurance that everything would be okay.

Then he killed himself.

"He took a gun to his head and blew his brains out," forensic psychologist Paula Orange said. "That left an indelible image on Shayne's outlook on life."

His suicide would leave the family in financial ruin. The papers would ridicule Mills, giving voice to all of the wild allegations of his mismanagement. The family would be left shamed and with nothing.

The effect was devastating on Shayne. She would go from being the richest girl in the school to being dirt poor.

Again.

Shayne just wanted to get away. She had entertained aspirations of being broadcast anchor, thinking that her beauty and speaking skills would lead to an easy gig. So she decided to move out of state for college. She would attend a university in Missouri where she would meet Kelly Lovera.

They would marry a year later.

The couple would have two children over the next five years despite being the polar opposites temperamentally.

Kelly was cool, calm and wanted a quiet life. He didn't embrace the partying lifestyle that Shayne wanted.

"Theirs was a union that is hard to comprehend," Orange said. "Kelly was not en route to becoming the next bank president. He was a twenty-year old student who was struggling. He wanted to be a math teacher. Shayne wanted to live a hedonistic lifestyle. She wanted to party and spend lavishly. Why they would get married defies explanation."

Bored in Missouri, Shayne would then convince Kelly to move back to her hometown in Tennessee. Kelly would consent to the move.

## A RETURN TO POVERTY

The couple would live in Sevierville which was thirteen miles north of her former luxury home in Gatlinburg. But it was light years away in terms of affluence as they were forced to rent out a small, one story townhouse.

The neighborhood they lived in was called "Frog Alley".

"A luxury once experienced becomes a necessity," Orange said. "Shayne had gotten used to living the high life. But married life, particularly one with of a lack of resources, would prove to be difficult for her."

"Frog Alley was a place for the working poor," Satterfield said. "To come back and live there would be extremely embarrassing for her."

Kelly's focus was not on making money. He was working on his master's degree in mathematics while he took a teaching position at Pellissippi College in Knoxville. Shayne would work various odd jobs to help the family make ends meet and was not happy about that.

"She had wild ambitions to become a news anchor," Orange said. "But she didn't do anything to make that happen. She wanted someone else to do all the work for her just like she experienced when her step-father financed her life."

## BOREDOM SETS IN

Shayne entertained neighbors for barbecues and poker nights. The problem is, the only people that seemed to come around were other men.

She was thoroughly bored with her marriage and began to have multiple affairs.

"She would flirt with men in full view of the children," Orange said. "Men would come over ostensibly to play cards. She would play 'footsie' with them underneath the poker table. She didn't want to be a mother and got bored with that act. She wanted to party, to be the rich wild girl that she was as a teenager. The idea of staying home with a boring math teacher and two needy children was anathema to her. She wanted a way out."

The affairs would occur in her apartment when Kelly was away. Different men would come and go at various hours.

"He's (Kelly) cramping my style," Shayne told one of her lovers. "And you're so much better than him."

"Thanks," her lover said with a grin.

"Do you know anything about how to poison someone?"

"Excuse me?"

"You know," Shayne said. "How certain poisons are undetectable."

Shayne would test the waters with her lovers. She would ask them about poisons in a joking manner. But then they would soon realize that she was serious. There was an ulterior motive to her affairs.

She wanted to find someone to kill her husband.

And she would find a willing assassin in Brett Rae.

THE NEXT DOOR NEIGHBOR

Brett was young and inexperienced with women. He had never encountered anyone like the sexy Shayne Lovera.

"Brett fell very hard for Shayne," Satterfield said. "Their affair started very quickly. And it was hot and heavy."

"Brett was a rich kid," Satterfield said. "His father was a newspaper publisher (Rick Rae, a Canadian publisher of the Sevier County newspaper). He was a well-to-do guy. He was just wild. He was just one of those people who was 'full-on' all of the time. He was up for anything."

And he was completely infatuated with Shayne.

Shayne set up Brett the same way she set up her other lovers. After a torrid session of lovemaking, she popped the question.

*Will you kill my husband?*

"I'll do anything for you," he told her with baited breath.

Shayne offered him a deal.

"If he were to get rid of Kelly," Satterfield said. "Then he would get her. That's what Brett wanted."

"Brett let his little head do the thinking for his big head," Orange said. "He was going to inherit money from his father so he had absolutely nothing to gain by killing Shayne's husband. Nothing except sex which of course if he had money, he would have more options than a narcissistic married woman. He simply did not have the life experience to see Shayne for what she was."

She would have a party on November $5^{th}$, 1994, an outdoor barbecue with gambling and drinking. Kelly left the party early and went to sleep on the couch.

Brett would be the last one to leave that evening. On his way out the door, they both noticed Kelly asleep on the couch.

"It was a spontaneous thing," Orange said. "They didn't have a murder weapon so they used whatever was immediately available. That would be the baseball bat of Kelly's son."

Kelly would then be bludgeoned to death.

"The plan was to put him in his own vehicle," Satterfield said. "And make it look like an accident."

Brett then dragged Kelly into his jeep and drove down Highway 14. He parked near an embankment and pushed the jeep down the side, watching it carom into a tree.

He then called one of his friends to pick him up.

Brett did not keep the news of the murder to himself. He would brag to two of his friends of what he had done.

"I put him (Kelly) over a hundred foot embankment," Brett said. "I fucked his wife and killed his ass. She told me I'd get more sex and more money if I get rid of him so I did."

Brett told his friends of the other methods he thought of using to kill Kelly but that he decided to beat him to death with the baseball bat then "stage a car crash."

FINDING THE BODY

**A pair of tourists would discover Kelly's black jeep below the road. Inside, they would see his bloodied dead body. Initially, they believed that he was the victim of an accident. They called the authorities and reported that it appeared as if his jeep had gone off the road and hit a tree**

Park Ranger Jerry Grubb was notified of the "accident" at the Great Smoky Mountains National Park.

The whole scene, however, looked suspicious from the get-go.

"Just wasn't any skid marks," Grubb said. "No disturbed gravel. There just wasn't any disturbance in that area."

Grubb looked inside the jeep and found the body of Kelly Lovera, laying in a pool of blood trailing toward the front seat. The blood should have been trailing behind the victim if he had, in fact, struck the tree head on.

Additionally, Kelly's injuries were not consistent with a car crash victim. The facial injuries appeared to be the result of a beating, not the impact of the jeep against the tree.

## MURDER ON THEIR HANDS

The autopsy would reveal that Kelly had been beaten to death and a homicide investigation ensued. Authorities would then visit Shayne's apartment and inform her of her husband's death.

She would go into hysterics, sobbing uncontrollably.

"Do you know why anyone would want to do this to him?" an investigator asked.

"He doesn't have any enemies!" she bawled.

But an officer would notice blood splatter on the glass of Kelly's diploma that was placed on a wall near the couch. They would obtain a search warrant and a crime team would arrive, spraying luminol over the apartment.

Luminol lightens up blood stains when a fluorescent ray is scanned over it.

"The whole living room lit up like a Christmas tree," Orange said. "That is when they knew they had the guilty party."

Detectives then began to question neighbors who all pointed their fingers at Brett Rae, the lover of Shayne.

Both Shayne and Brett were arrested and charged with first-degree premeditated murder.

Brett would confess quickly. He admitted to using the baseball bat and then staging the car wreck. He would be represented by Robert Ritchie who would prep him for the murder trial for nearly three months. Ritchie, however, would notice that Brett was completely obsessed with Shayne. He then turned the case over to Robert Ogle but two weeks before the trial Alan Feltes was brought in as Brett was given joint representation.

"His attorneys were flabbergasted at his refusal to give up Shayne," Orange said. "He was truly in love with her and wanted to protect her even if it meant incriminating himself."

"I did it," Brett insisted. "Just leave her out of it."

Feltes told Brett that there was no way he could win the case with all of the evidence stacked against him. The only thing Brett cared about was putting Shayne in jeopardy.

THE TRIAL

Park Ranger Jerry Grubb would testify against the killing duo, presenting the forensic evidence found at the home and jeep. Friends and family would testify that both Shayne and Brett had bragged to them about what they had done.

Going in desperation mode, Shayne would then take the stand. She wanted to tell her version of what happened that night.

"Brett had stopped by to talk to me when Kelly came out and confronted him," Shayne said. "They began fighting and Brett picked up a baseball bat. He swung it only to keep Kelly away. But then he accidentally hit him and killed him."

Shayne would go on to say that she didn't witness any of this. She was asleep and really knew nothing that happened.

"Brett and I were not lovers," Shayne said. "We were nothing more than neighbors. It was a case of fatal attraction. He had a thing for me and wanted to kill my husband."

She didn't know, however, that when both she and Brett were released on bail they were followed by a Siever County Sheriff. He followed them into the mountains and saw them having intercourse in the woods.

When Shayne was confronted with this evidence, she tried to regroup.

"I had sex with Brett," Shayne said. "But only because I had to. He threatened to involve me in the murder plot. My purpose in going there was trying to save what little bit of life I had left at that point."

The explanation did not go over well with the jury. It took them only an hour and a half to return with a guilty verdict.

OFF TO JAIL

On January 29th, 1996, both Shayne and Brett would be convicted of Kelly's murder. They would not be given the death penalty, however. The prosecution wanted a sentence of life without parole.

Feltes approached by the attorneys for Shayne. They stated that a plea agreement would be possible but it would have to be a package deal with Brett.

Feltes advised Brett to take the deal as the plea agreement would guarantee him a life sentence with possibility of parole. If he didn't take the deal, the odds would be that he would be facing life without parole.

"Just don't do anything to hurt Shayne," Brett said. "I want to see her."

"What?"

"I want to see her before I take the deal."

Brett would persist in wanting to see Shayne. Instead he would take the deal.

"His attorneys described him as having the saddest eyes they had ever seen in a courtroom," Orange said. "He was truly in love with Shayne. She, on the other hand, threw him under the bus. She was willing to say whatever it took to get herself off and it backfired."

THE AFTERMATH

Kelly's children would be placed into the care of his parents. Brett and Shayne would receive life with parole after twenty-five years.

Brett would later try to appeal his sentencing despite agreeing to a plea bargain which barred him from doing so.

His claim would be rejected.

Ray would write that "his trial was ineffective for encouraging him to accept the state's offer of life with possibility of parole; failing to prepare for mitigating circumstances at the sentencing phase; failing to properly conduct a pre-trial investigation; failing to adequately consult with him during critical stages of the proceedings; failing to advise him of his rights to direct appeal and collateral attack of his conviction; deficient performance of counsel at trial; his guilty plea was coerced and involuntary; and his conviction is void as violating the protection against double jeopardy."

"He had conceded his guilt during the guilty plea hearing and that his attorneys did the best they could...he made these admissions only because the attorneys instructed him to do so and although he agreed that he believed himself to be guilty of first degree murder at the time of his plea, he now retracts that admission."

Brett's attorney Feltes would dispute his allegations, stating that he "never had any problem with Brett being incoherent or not understanding anything he was told or advised."

Both Brett and Shayne remain in prison, waiting to be paroled in 2025.

# HUSBAND KILLER : THE TRUE STORY OF MARY WINKLER

89

JAMES FALCON

## The Case of Mary Winkler

Mary Winkler, at first appearances, would seem to be an altogether normal woman. So too did her family, with a husband who was a Church minister and three young children, girls aged just eight, six and one.

The family lived in Selmer, Tenn., a small town occupied by around 4,500 people, according to the 2015 census. The town is situated to the south west of the state. Not much has happened in Selmer; the most famous person to have been born there was Chad Harville, former pitcher for the Oakland A's, and for one year, the Red Sox. He achieved a 4-9 win-loss record over his career in the MLB.

Today, the most famous- or infamous- person to have come from Selmer is Mary Winkler. In 2006, Mary sparked a border-crossing manhunt, and a court case followed nationwide. She had killed her husband with a shot to the back from the family's shotgun. But it was the gripping, and at times bizarre, court case which gripped the attention of the nation.

### Matthew dead, Mary and the family Missing

The date was March 6$^{\text{th}}$, 2007. It was a Tuesday like any other. Mary and Matthew were at home all day together, although Matthew was due to give a sermon that evening.

It was actually members of Matthew's congregation who found his body that night. They had visited his home to check up on him after he had missed the service he was set to give; instead, they found him lying dead, having been shot in the back.

There was no sign of Mary or any of their children at the home, and as such, they were reported missing. The authorities quickly sent out an Amber Alert, since nobody had any idea what could have happened to them, or where they might be. Family and friends had no information to provide police on their whereabouts.

There was every chance that the family had been kidnapped or murdered, and their bodies disposed of elsewhere, although police could not identify a break in, and had no reason to believe that anything of value had been stolen.

It was only a day later that she was arrested in Alabama, having run from the family home with her young children. They were found 350 miles away from home, at Orange Beach, and in the back seat of the van was the family's shotgun. It was certainly suspicious; but what reason could Mary have possibly had for committing such a crime?

**The Trial**

In the build up to the case going to trial, public interest ramped up. Speculation had been rife about why Mary would have murdered her husband, a seemingly nice, well respected member of the local community. Perhaps either one of them had had an affair, and Matthew had been killed in a crime of passion. Or maybe he had been killed for an insurance claim?

As such, the press reported every step of the story as it came out during the hearing. The trial began when a Tennessee Bureau of Investigation Agent John Mehr read a statement that Mary had made very soon after her arrest. In it, Mary claimed that the couple had been arguing about their family finances, before Mary had shot her husband with their 12 gauge shotgun. She had said that the last thing she had wanted was to actually murder her husband, but she had been brandishing the gun in an effort to convince him to work through their problems, together. The argument had been ongoing throughout the day, and Mary had finally snapped, resorting to drastic measures to be able to convince him. She had never intended to kill him: she had said in the statement, 'I don't want this at all. I don't want any of this to be, at all.'

The statement continued on, and Mary claimed that they had argued often and argued fiercely. 'He had really been on me lately,' Mary had said, 'criticizing me for things- the way I walk, I eat, everything. It was just building up to a point. I was tired of it. I guess I got to a point and snapped.'

At first glance, it would seem that Mary had simply lost her composure, become angry, and killed her husband 'as the red mist had descended'. But after their initial statement, Mary's attorney indicated that there was much more that would come out about Matthew's behaviour when she testified which would help to explain her actions. Clearly, there were more problems with their marriage than the occasional, albeit fierce, argument.

## Mary's Crime

The case for the prosecution wasted no time in painting Mary as a cold blooded killer, who left her husband to die without remorse. Admittedly, the plain facts of the case made Mary seem unbelievably guilty. The prosecution relied on several of these facts in their attempt to convince the jury of Mary's guilt for the charge of murder.

Mary had disconnected the phone immediately after she shot her husband, stopping him from being able to call the emergency services, or receive any calls that may have come in. This suggested that Mary had been in full control of her actions, not panicking, since it is unlikely that somebody in a state of anxiety would think to disconnect the phone.

The fact that Mary had attempted to flee to Orange Beach, Alabama, was also a key point for the prosecution. Immediately after Matthew's death, Mary had taken the family minivan to the beach, with her three children. Later on in her defence, Mary would claim that she ran because '[n]obody would believe me, and they'd take the girls away and put me away.' Certainly, in many murder cases, the fact that the defendant flees the scene is a certain indicator of guilt.

The family's daughter Patricia testified that she couldn't understand her mother's actions. All that she knew was that she had heard a 'big boom', and the sound of something heavy hitting the floor. She quickly ran to the bedroom to see her father on the floor, and her mother holding the shotgun. She had no idea what could possibly have provoked her mother to shoot him.

Another sticking point was that the family finances had been 'in shambles' just before the murder had taken place. This had led Mary to become embroiled in what is called a 'check kiting' scam. In it, she had received checks from unidentified accounts in Canada and Nigeria, and had ultimately fallen to a financial scam that had lost the family money. Prosecutors claimed that this could have somehow instigated the argument that led to Matthew's death, and that Mary had felt as if she had no way out of the scam.

They also jumped on the fact that in an initial conversation with investigators, Mary had told them that their marriage was a happy one, and that '[t]here's no poor me. I'm in control.' They clearly wanted to paint a picture of Mary as remorseless, deceitful, and smarter than she looked.

**The Cross-examination**

During her cross-examination in court, Mary stated that she didn't remember grabbing the gun from the closet in which it was kept. What she did remember was that 'something went off', 'hearing a loud boom', and that 'it wasn't as loud as I thought it would be.' She did admit that she had shot her husband. Matthew rolled from the bed- upon which he had been lying as they had argued- and dropped to the floor. Mary described smelling gunpowder.

Prosecutor Walter Freeland asked her whether she understood that 'pulling a trigger is what makes it go boom', to which she replied that she did.

Matthew asked her why she had snapped and shot him. She could only say 'I'm sorry.' The shotgun blast had been inflicted from behind, directly into Matthew's back, and had caused severe damage to his organs and spine. According to prosecutors, he had in fact still been alive as Mary had run from the house.

But these simple facts were far from the end of the story, as Mary was to reveal.

**Appearances and Revelations**

At first, Mary spoke of her husband not in the past tense, but in the present, as if she couldn't quite understand how final her actions really had been. In reminiscing about happier times, Mary told the court that her husband was an intelligent, social man, and that the family had shared many 'good times' together. She also seemed to enjoy talking about her children, and the happiness they brought her.

This happy family life, however, was simply one side of the marriage. Mary's attorney stated that '[w]hat went on behind their closed doors is going to have to be told ... Some of what we've got from the state of Tennessee touches on sexual abuse.' Their defence was that Matthew had made Mary's life a 'living hell': '[w]e will show you proof that he would destroy objects that she loved, he would isolate her from her family and he would abuse her not just verbally, not just emotional and not just physically—in other ways, too.'

Just before the murder, Mary claimed that Matthew had been threatening their children and even attempted to throttle their infant daughter, Breanna. He had been shouting, angry, because he had wanted a son. As the case went on, it became obvious that this was only the tip of the iceberg, however, and more and more sordid details of their home life would come to light.

Matthew, Mary claimed, was a violent, abusive husband. Shortly after their marriage, he ordered her to stop socialising with any of her family and friends (a common tactic among abusive spouses in order to further isolate their partners from potential help). Winkler's sisters described how Mary seemed stuck in her marriage, unhappy, but unable to leave. In an interview, they said that 'As the years went on, she seemed to be nervous to show love towards us.'

Mary was commonly 'screamed and hollered' at by her husband. 'He just flailed. He's a big guy and he was just all over ... He'd point his finger inches away from my nose. Whatever he was upset about, it was my fault,' Mary had said. It could be over anything: 'I was fat, my hair wasn't right, the girls, if something went wrong, it was my fault. I didn't know when it was coming.' Mary described her situation as one familiar to abused wives and husbands across America.

Her attorney, Steve Farese, provided further information based on his conversations with Mary. She had needed her husband's permission for everything, even for getting her hair cut. 'This was constant, and she lived a life where she walked on eggshells.' This abuse, he said, had given Mary symptoms of post traumatic stress disorder, simply because 'she didn't know what was going to happen next.' Furthermore, a psychologist testified as part of Mary's defence, saying that her symptoms were those of clinical depression and PTSD.

During her time on the stand, Mary also claimed that Matthew had forced her to watch pornography with him, and that he had bought her several 'slutty' costumes for sex, which she normally would never have worn, but for fear of her husband. If she refused, Matthew wouldn't hesitate to get physical, hitting her or even using his belt to whip her. Mary famously produced a wig and a pair of white high heels in the witness box during her cross-examination to show the court evidence of Matthew's other side.

Mary stated that she was never happy watching pornography, dressing up in sexy outfits or performing the sex acts that Matthew wanted. She went along with his ideas, however, because she didn't dare face his reaction if she didn't. 'I'd just do anything to help him stay happy.' Throughout these revelations, Mary was visibly embarrassed and uncomfortable. Clearly she would have preferred that none of them had ever come to light; but Mary felt it necessary to brave what her neighbors, and the nation, might think in order to clear her name and justify her actions.

Mary's family had been quick to corroborate her side of the story. Her father, Clark Freeman, had spoken out through Good Morning America and detailed the 'physical, mental, verbal' abuse that his daughter had suffered. Other friends came forward during the court case, and gave similar verdicts on their relationship. A friend of Mary's,

Rudie Thomsen, said that '[o]ne Sunday, Mary came into the church and I looked at her and she had a black eye.' Similarly, Mary's friend Amy Redmon agreed that Matthew had been controlling: '[h]e was an authority figure, and he made the decisions basically. It was obvious.'

Conversely, Matthew's family denied that their son had been anything like Mary had depicted in her defence testimony. Matthew's father, Charles Daniel Winkler, said that his son was a kind, gentle man, who could have done nothing to justify what the defence was claiming. Diane spoke several times during the trial, lashing out at Mary: 'You've never told your girls you're sorry! Don't you think you at least owe them that?'

The dramatic story of a supposedly kindly, gentle church minister having such a sordid, cruel and abusive hidden life gripped America. The case was covered extensively on all major networks, discussed on late night panel shows

**The Jury's Verdict**

While the prosecutors had tried to convince the jury to convict her on a charge of first degree murder, they were unsuccessful. The jury came to their verdict by April, that year. It took them eight hours to deliberate their way to the decision; this mirrored the response of the nation, which was similarly undecided on just what punishment Mary really deserved.

Mary was found guilty of voluntary manslaughter, a charge which carries a far more lenient sentence than murder. While murderers can receive full life sentences, and in certain states receive the death penalty, the maximum sentence for voluntary manslaughter is only 6 years.

Mary showed little emotion at the verdict, but did embrace each of her relatives afterwards. In a show of support, her family had been sat in the row behind her, and all linked arms with one another to demonstrate their solidarity. Afterwards, she was taken back into custody to await sentencing.

Mary's attorney stated afterwards that Mary's testimony had been central in securing the more lenient sentence. 'I think Mary's testimony was integral in this decision. They had to hear it from Mary', Farese told the press. 'They judged her credibility and they saw that she had an abusive relationship and they made their judgment based upon that.'

For Mary, the most important implication of the verdict was that she could finally begin to think of being reunited with her children. Speaking on her behalf after the trial, Farese continued: 'We would like to do so many things to open up communication between Mary and the paternal grandparents and to get the children out of this cycle of constant upheaval over this terrible tragic event.' But the question of how long she would be in prison remained.

Mary's sentencing was scheduled for May 18$^{th}$, at which point both Mary and the prosecution would have a final chance to address the court before the judge decided on the final jail term. However, the situation looked positive for Mary. Not only would the five months that she had been imprisoned awaiting trial be taken into consideration, but the judge had indicated that alternatives to incarceration would be on the table. Perhaps Mary could avoid jail time altogether.

**Sentencing: The Trial at an End**

Due to a scheduling error, the hearing took place around three weeks late, on June 8$^{th}$.

Mary took to the stand one last time to plead for mercy. She read aloud from a prepared statement, telling Matthew's family of her sorrow and remorse for her actions. She was 'so sorry that this had happened', and would 'always miss and love' her husband. 'I ask for mercy and understanding, but I know whatever decision you reach today will be right ... I ask you to please let me go home today and be with my children.' Tabitha Freeman- Mary's sister- had also pleaded for leniency, in particular to let Mary be reunited with her children. She went as far as calling Mary 'the best example of a good person I can think of'.

Members of Matthew's family, too, took to the stand to plead their case for the prosecution. Charles and his wife were clearly hurt and in disbelief at Mary's actions both in murdering their son, and believed that Mary had purposefully smeared his name at trial. 'The monster that you have painted for the world to see? I don't think that monster existed,' Diane Winkler had said.

After speaking their pieces, all that Mary, her family, and Matthew's parents could do was wait until the judge's decision. The trial- as well as the very public 'trial' that Mary had been through in the media- was finally at an end.

The defence had requested that Mary be granted full probation, or judicial diversion, both outcomes which would have meant that Mary would spent no further time in prison, and even that her record would be cleared of wrongdoing altogether. This request was denied.

After recess, Mary was told that she would spend 3 years in prison for her crime. But Circuit Judge J. Weber McCraw reduced that amount to just 210 days total in prison before she would be allowed to leave on probation. She also had that sentence reduced further, due to the fact that she had spent five months incarcerated waiting for trial.

Moreover, that time would be spent not in jail, but in a mental health centre in Tennessee. There, she would receive treatment for both her depression and post traumatic stress disorder. After such a long ordeal, with the prosecution fighting to either put Mary on death row or to imprison her indefinitely, it seemed that she had gotten off with hardly a slap on the wrist.

Steve Farese branded the sentence 'a victory': '[s]he could be in prison for life, and that's what everybody thought she was headed for to begin with.' Her other attorney, Leslie Ballin, said '[s]he'll be able to get out and fight the battle she wants to, and that is to get her children back.' Mary could finally think about the future again.

But certain signs indicated that it would not be as easy to reconcile with her children and family as she might hope. Matthew's family left the courtroom without making a comment to the press, as did the prosecution, clearly disappointed in the verdict. They gave no indication that they would be happy to open dialogue about Mary's daughters- not with the woman whom they believed to have murdered their son in cold blood.

### The aftermath of Mary's release

Mary was released on August 14th, 2007. She had only been sentenced the previous June.

Upon her release, her lawyer informed the press that Mary would not be speaking with them, to maintain her privacy. During her time in the mental health facility, Mary could finally begin her attempt to win full custody of her three daughters, and she was still fighting this case at the time of her release. She had not seen her children, apart from Patricia's brief testimony as part of the case, for over a year. Throughout the case, and after Mary's release, her children were staying with Matthew's family.

Moreover, she was still fighting a $2 million dollar civil lawsuit filed by Matthew's parents. They also took legal measures, which, if successful, would have meant that the custody of Mary's children remained with them.

After her release, Mary seemed happier to her family and friends. From an outside perspective, it could be easy to claim that this was just as much due to her happiness at avoiding a jail sentence as it was to her being rid of an abuser. She was in fact living with friends at first after her release, and went back to work at a dry cleaners in McMinnville, Tenn., 200 miles from Selmer.

In the same interview as was mentioned before, Mary's sisters agreed that she had changed entirely. After years of shyness, Mary seeming unable or unwilling to show love to them for fear of her husband's violence, she seemed to finally be able to open up. 'Now it's back to the old Mary [who] loves us and doesn't care to come and hug us and gives us a kiss on the cheek.'

Since then, Mary lived in McMinnville. She has moved between jobs, working at the dry cleaners, before starting work at a nursery. She briefly dated the brother of one of her most vocal supporters, Paul Pillow; afterwards, she moved in with Wayne Cantrell, a preacher living in Smithville nearby.

Mary regained custody of her three children in 2008, but by 2010, received the news that she had multiple sclerosis. Her diagnosis came at the worst time, as she was settling down in her new life; she had not long started medical school with the desire to become a nurse, and had to quit since the work would be too demanding. She hasn't returned to work since.

One comfort for Mary was that Matthew's parents seemed close to being able to forgive her. After her diagnosis, they gave Mary some time off from parenting by taking care of the children for a weekend, which soon turned into several months. Daniel Winkler has preached several times since the events on the topic of forgiveness, although when asked by local press why he chose the topic, he has refused to answer, presumably preferring to keep those details private.

Mary, too, preferred to put the past behind her. In an interview with WAFF 48, the NBC affiliate in Huntsville AL., she stated how she would prefer to stay out of the limelight, particularly for the sake of her girls. 'Whatever reason people have any problem with me, that's fine. Everybody's entitled to their opinion, but these girls are treated for who they are, not because of what their mother's done ... They're three very fine young ladies'.

**Concluding Thoughts**

Some members of the public reacted with disgust at the abnormally short sentence that Mary was given, and questioned whether a husband would have been given the same leniency as Mary was. Men's rights activist Glenn Sacks publicly questioned whether a man would have been shown such leniency, and pointed to the case of Scott Peterson (who received the death penalty for the murder of his pregnant wife) to indicate that no, a man would not. He also argued that the idea of abuse had been widened to include simple criticism, and should therefore not necessarily be used as defence of murder.

Conversely, there have been many women put in prison for murdering their abusive husbands, some for much longer than Mary Winkler. The 'battered woman defense', or the preferred terminology today of 'battering and its effects', is not a genuine legal defence in itself; it can, however, be used to convince a court of diminished responsibility. Its effectiveness is due to the sympathy that it elicits from jurors, who can be convinced that abuse is a form of provocation, and the murder a form of self defense. Under this defense, Mary's short sentence makes sense.

The case has remained a touch stone with regards to spousal abuse in the U.S. A made-for-TV movie, 'The Pastor's Wife', was released in 2011. It was based on the book of the same title, written by Dianne Fanning, an award winning crime writer. The story was changed somewhat, with the inclusion of a financial subplot involving tax fraud. However, it also made use of real life interviews with people who knew the Winklers- including Matthew's parents. His mother revealed that she could never believe Mary's story. Charles admitted that Mary's story could be true, and that he could forgive her if she confessed her purposeful intention to murder Matthew.

As for the community in which the family had lived, the reaction was largely one of forgiveness. According to members of that community, the town's 'Christian roots and ... its tendency to give people the benefit of the doubt' meant that they took Mary at her word. Mary's quite life in McMinnville and Smithville similarly shows that the American public would rather leave her and her family alone after their painful ordeal.

# TRACEY GRISSOM

Claiming to be a victim of rape and other abuses, a distraught Tracey Grissom would travel to her ex-husband Hunter's workplace and shoot him six times in the back, receiving a twenty-five-year life sentence for his murder.

Her defense attorney would argue that Tracey was motivated by post-traumatic stress disorder caused by her Hunter's constant abuse and sexual assaults. One jury member had even asked the judge to be lenient in her sentencing as they were not allowed to hear details of her Hunter's alleged abuses (beatings, rape, sodomy).

But what really happened in the years that led up to May 15th, 2012? Was she in fact the victim of years of abuse by a psychotic husband? Or did she want to cash in on his $100,000 life insurance policy?

INSTANT ATTRACTION

The couple would meet during a dinner party in 2003 in Tuscaloosa, Alabama. Tracey was twenty-one years old and going through a divorce. She had a son, James Michael, from the previous marriage.

Family and friends would describe the union as "love at first sight." Hunter was blown away by the young Tracey's blue eyes and facial beauty.

"For him, it was love at first sight," crime author William Phelps said. "She was gorgeous."

A whirlwind courtship would ensue and the couple would elope in 2004.

"In the beginning, it was good," Tracey told CBS' 48 hours. "We had a friendship. Just your normal, honeymoon phase marriage."

"He was fun," Tracey said. "And he was attractive."

Hunter was two years younger than Tracey, however, and his mother felt that he had jumped the gun too early in the relationship.

Her words proved to be prophetic as after only eight months into the marriage, the marriage went south.

According to Tracey, their marital problems began with Hunter's drug addiction.

"I had caught him smoking marijuana," Tracey said. "Doing illegal things could cause a problem and I couldn't risk losing my son over."

Tracey claimed that she threatened her new spouse with a divorce but Hunter gave her his word that he would stop with his drug use. She stated that the relationship improved and the decided to start a construction company together.

"I took out an equity line to start a company," Tracey said. "Which was Grissom Construction. It was all in my name."

Hunter specialized in building elaborate boat docks. He had an artistic eye and could do docks, stairs, and other accouterments. The business began to grow in short order.

"They're going to take on the world," Phelps said. "They're going to be entrepreneurs and they're gonna make it."

They then had a daughter of their own, Anna Grace. The child was a long time coming for the couple. They had been trying for a long time as Tracey had five miscarriages before Anna Grace was born.

"She was premature," Tracey recalled. "Her heart and lungs were not developed. A very stressful time."

Behind closed doors things were rocky. On the surface, however, things looked good. They had a young family and were making money.

"All-American family," Phelps said. "White-picket fence. The whole nine yards. Middle-class. Suburbia. Maybe the Prince Charming that she's been waiting for."

But again, this was only on the surface. Tracey harbored secrets of her own. One of which was her own addiction to prescription drugs.

"Psychologically, there's something going on here," Phelps said. "There's something going on behind those beautiful eyes and it ain't good."

Tracey would often turn on on the children, showing off her temper. Then she would turn on Hunter.

"This would cause friction in the marriage," Phelps said. "And where there's friction, there's fire."

SETTING THE STAGE

Tracey would later state that Hunter would "act strangely" shortly before she filed divorce. She was a registered nurse and gave him an over-the-counter drug test. According to her, Hunter tested posted for marijuana, Oxycontin, opiates, and methamphetamine.

Hunter would later be arrested for marijuana possession but his family would insist that he never did the harder drugs.

Tracey would file for divorce in the summer of 2010 after six years of marriage. According to her, this would prompt physical abuse from Hunter.

Hunter had to move out but their divorce agreement would allow him access to the home.

"In September of 2010," Tracey recalled. "That was the first time he physically hit me. It (the abuse) got progressively worse. He had made the comments that if I told anybody he would kill me. I believed him."

Hunter' co-workers and family members would have a different take on the situation, however. His co-workers remembered a time when she tracked him down at one of the jobs and made a scene.

"She's screaming, jumping on him," Hunter's co-worker said. "Said something about him having another girlfriend and used the expression about, 'You are mine. I'll kill you. I'll kill you. You are mine."

"She's borderline demonic," Hunter's mother said. " mean, I absolutely believe—that she is that troubled."

Hunter's family continued to believe that he did not abuse Tracey.

"He did not have an abusive, an angry bone in his body," Hunter's aunt Gina said. "In fact, we kind of laughed at him because he was too laid-back."

The divorce was finalized in October of 2010.

EVIDENCE OF ABUSE?

Loran Richards was the first of Tracey's friends to notice the minor injuries on her body. She would inquire about the bruises but the answers she received were always evasive. Seeing Tracey with a black eye, however, forced her to try and get more answers.

"I said, Tracey, you may have terrible luck," Richards recalled. "But nobody is so unlucky that they trip, fall down the stairs, and hit their face on a baseball in the eye socket. So don't give me a lame excuse. You don't have to give me any excuse, but let's take a picture."

Tracey broke down. She gave her friend all of the grisly details, detailing the abuse she suffered at the hands of Hunter. Loran then became her advocate, taking pictures of Tracey's injuries. She would later state that she saw blood stains and other signs of abuse at Tracey's home.

THAT FATEFUL NIGHT

Now divorced, Hunter would arrive at Tracey's home on November 22nd, 2010.

According to Tracey, he then became enraged when Tracey told him that she had spent the night with a new lover.

"He told me that he was gonna kill me," Tracey recalled. Tracey stated that she tried to escape, running into the closet in order to "get away from the kids and to pray." Tracey's eleven-year-old son from a previous relationship was in the home as was the four-year-old daughter they have together.

Hunter caught up with her and knocked her to the ground. He tied a belt around her ankles and then began choking her.

Half-conscious, Tracey alleged to have been raped and sodomized.

The brutal attack would leave Tracey unconscious. She would wake up the next morning on the bathroom floor.

"I called Hunter," Tracey recalled. "I told him that I was bleeding and that I was hurt and that I needed help. And he told me, 'Fuck you. I hope you die.'"

Tracey wound up in the emergency room after the attack. Hospital records would show that she had a laceration on her head, bruises, and ligature marks on her feet.

Tracey would then be referred to the Turning Point domestic violence center.

Marian Waters would describe Tracey's injuries as among the worst she had ever seen in a twenty-year career.

Waters would testify that Tracey had suffered a horrific assault. She described her mental state as typical of someone who had just been raped; fearful, jumpy, fearing for her life.

Tracey had suffered a hematoma on her side that was the side of a grapefruit. She also claimed to have experienced rectal nerve damage which would require surgery as well as torn vaginal muscles requiring her to have a hysterectomy.

Police were called and Hunter would be arrested for rape, sodomy, kidnapping and domestic violence.

"And at that point, I feared for my life," Tracey recalled. "And I feared for my children's life."

A HIDDEN AGENDA

Hunter would be freed on bail but Tracey got a restraining order against him. She bought a gun and did not go anywhere unarmed.

She took photos of her injuries on the night of the alleged attack and texted them to Loran. Later, they would take more pictures.

Angered, Hunter would stop paying her spousal and child support. Tracey, however, may have had another scenario in mind for obtaining money.

She had forced Hunter to take out a $103,000 life insurance policy around the time their daughter was born.

On May 24, 2012, the day before Tracey shot Hunter, she would place a call to MetLife that was recorded.

"Thank you for calling MetLife, this is Pam. May I please have your name?"

"Tracey Grissom."

Tracey would then explain that she was angry that her husband stopped making payments on his policy. During their divorce proceedings, he had agreed to continue paying the premiums. Tracey stated she was calling to make sure that they had the correct address on file.

"Is there anything else I can do for you today?

"That's gonna be it!" Tracey said, hanging up.

"Well, May 14th was just like any other day," Tracey said, explaining the call to the insurance company. "However, I had moved four different times. Me and my children were running. We were running from Hunter. So I had called the company to let them know that they had my old address and to make an address change."

FALSE RAPE?

Shelly Standridge was hired by Hunter to defend him in the rape case. She would state that Hunter denied raping or even assaulting Tracey that night. Hunter did, however, admit to the fact that he and his wife had consensual sex that night...Rough consensual sex.

"So that night," Standridge said. "Hunter said that she was depressed and claiming she was going to kill herself. She was saying she wanted their relationship to work."

So she undressed in front of him. Her beauty was always impossible for Hunter to resist.

The two had sex despite Hunter having a new girlfriend at home.

Hunter's aunt, Gina, believed that Tracey wanted to kill Hunter before the rape case went to court.

"He had a new girlfriend, he was living with her," Phelps said. "He was moving on with his life. Hunter would claim that Tracey was jealous, obsessive, even stalked them."

"Hunter had moved on," Hunter's aunt said. "There was some court dates coming up that would prove that Hunter was innocent. There were court dates coming up that he would get visitation to his daughter. She had a lot to lose."

Tracey was on the anti-anxiety drug Klonopin. Hunter would tell his attorney that Tracey would take more than her prescribed dose. Because of this, she fell and cut her head. Hunter would then leave the house around 10:30 pm and go to his father's house. Tracey would call him hours later, at 3:20 am.

Hunter would state that Tracey had called to threaten him. She told him if he didn't want the responsibility of the children then she would make it where he would never be able to see them again.

Hunter's attorney did not know what Tracey's motive was for crying rape. She was very upset that he had a girlfriend.

MORE LIES...

Hunter would be arrested nearly twelve hours later, to his total shock.

Tracey would give her side of the story to the police which later is proven to be false.

She would tell police that Hunter had thrown her against the bathtub around 10 pm and claim to be unconscious until 4 am the next morning.

"But her phone records show she was on the phone all night, so she was never unconscious," Standridge said. "She was also using her data at 10:42 that night. She was using it again at 10:50 that night. ... She sends a text to her boyfriend at 1:49 am. She sends a text to her friend at 2:07 am. She sends another text to her boyfriend at 2:07 am."

Tracey would blame the calls on Hunter.

"All I do know is I was not the only person using my phone that night," Tracey said, suggesting that Hunter used her phone.

Medical records would show that Tracey's head wound was "purely superficial".

Only one suture was needed.

Furthermore, there was nothing on the medical record to support the fact that Tracey experienced vaginal and rectal tears. She did have bruises on her ankle and legs but the photos taken by police at the emergency room would not resemble the same photos that Tracey and her friend Loran would take days later. In the photos taken at the emergency room, an area of Tracey's body has no bruises. Days later, there is discoloration.

Tracey's attorney would blame the discrepancy on "blood thinners" which would cause Tracey to bruise easily.

There was also a discrepancy in her phone records. She would take a photo of her inner thigh, a deep bruise. This area of her body was not photographed by police during her emergency room visit. But on December 9th, almost two weeks later, Tracey took a photo of her inner thigh with the deep bruise

"He (Hunter) told me that he would make it to where nobody would ever want me," Tracey said after a 2010 attack. "I didn't report it because I thought he would kill me."

THE FINAL STRAW

Tracey woke up pissed on May 15th, 2012.

Hunter had been ordered to pay $2,100 a month for the rest of his life. He was not complying with the court order claiming that he was "out of work."

Tracey stated that she was on her way to a job interview when she saw a Grissom Construction sign out of the corner of her eye.

She stated that her initial plan was to take a photograph of Hunter at the job site in order to show proof that he was working as part of her litigation.

"I was getting ready to take the picture and when I looked up he was standing almost directly towards the front of the boat trailer," Tracey said. "He was looking back directly at me. He had this face, that's like mean - just, I don't know how to describe it. I mean, I see it over and over like it's right there all the time. He flipped me the bird, which to me was kinda like, 'Yeah I'm workin. Screw you.' And at that point, I panicked. At that point, I didn't know what else to do except to defend myself."

Tracey started firing. The first shot hit Hunter in the arm. He started to run and she fired again repeatedly. One of the bullets punctured Hunter's heart and he died of massive internal bleeding.

William Dockery was working with Hunter and was an eyewitness to the shooting. Hunter had turned to Dockery before the shooting and told him to "call the law". Before Dockery could pick up his cell phone, Tracey had commenced shooting.

Tracey then pulled out her own cell phone and called the cops on herself. She tearfully described that she had just murdered her husband.

CONFESSION

Tracey told detectives exactly what was going through her mind when she came upon Hunter at the construction site.

"Tell me about what happened," the detective said. "What led up to...what's going on."

"In November of 2010, he beat me unconscious and raped me...and, and left me for dead....and, and I finally pressed charges against him and he told me that he would make my life a living hell...and that's what he's done."

"What, what happened this morning that led up to you going..."

"I was going to work and I saw him...and he's been claiming that he-he's not working. And, so I pulled in there to take a picture of him...cause it was the truck that's still in my name...and the boat that's still in my name...and the trailer that's still in my name...He just stared at me and flipped me off...and I just went in there and shot him...I just shot him, I shot him, and I shot him."

Tracey would be distraught and tearful during her interrogation room confession. A few weeks later, however, she would call the insurance company to let them know that Hunter had died.

"Well, I was actually calling because I didn't know what I needed to do ... Hunter passed away May 15th and I actually am going a court case right now because it was due to self-defense..."

Hunter's family went ballistic over this. Tracey would claim that she had no money but she continued to pay his life insurance premiums.

"Even through the times when she's screamin' that she's destitute and has no money ... she continued to pay life insurance premium," Hunter's mother said.

"I don't think my sister concocted a story," Tracey's sister said. "Just so she could get insurance money. ... But that's all they (the prosecution) had."

THE TRIAL

Tracey's allegations of rape and sodomy would not be allowed in court testimony. She was allowed, however, to detail the effects of Hunter's abuse on her were.

Taking the stand, Tracey would lift up her shirt in court and show herself wearing a colostomy bag. She stated that she had undergone several surgeries after her husband's daily rapes wherein she suffered permanent rectal and vaginal damage.

Hunter's family was then allowed to speak at the hearing.

"This tremendous loss has changed me," Hunter's mother, Melanie Garner said. "And I don't know how to change back."

Chloe, Hunter's sister, had a victim's services officer read her letter in court.

"Tracey is psychotic," Chloe wrote. "She is the most selfish person human being on this earth."

"Every mother should pray every night that your son doesn't fall in love with someone like Tracey," Hunter's aunt, Gina Grissom said. "There have been lots of allegations against Hunter. We've never believed anything that has come out of her (Tracey's) mouth."

His aunt then looked directly at Tracey.

"Hunter was proud of his name. Why would you still choose to use our name, and bring it down?" suggesting that if Tracey hated him so much why didn't she go revert to her maiden name after the divorce.

The jurors would find Tracey guilty of murder. She would be sentenced to twenty-five years in prison.

One of the jurors, Janice Kelly, would contact Grissom's attorney Warren Freeman the morning after the trial. She had remorse over her decision and said that she wouldn't have convicted her had they had the rapes and abuse allegations been introduced as evidence.

"I feel I made a mistake," Kelly said. "If I had to do it over again, we'd have had a hung jury. We didn't get her side. She did not get a fair trial."

"We voted to convict because there was no dispute that Tracey shot Hunter," the jury foreman wrote in a letter that was addressed in the courthouse. "Jurors didn't believe prosecutor claims that she did it in order to collect a life insurance policy. We felt the shooting was a crime of passion, not for financial gain and that she should be sentenced accordingly. I wish we had seen evidence of the rape allegation. We feel that she just 'lost it.'"

"It's not fair, it's not fair!" Tracey sobbed as she was led out of the courthouse and to jail.

"We think the sentencing was too harsh," Tracey's attorney Warren Freeman said. "Considering you have the foreperson of the jury actually saying, we don't feel like she should be punished according to being found guilty of murder. Let's just say that there will be a basis for a new trial, and part of it will be something that the jurors saw that they weren't supposed to see and I'm going to just leave it at that until I file my motion."

"My son died running for his life," Hunter's mother said. "I don't know what was running through his mind but I hear him say 'momma.'"

"People who think that I murdered him in cold blood," Tracey said. "Either don't know the whole story or don't know everything that's happened.

Tracey was asked on CBS' 48 hours if she regretted pulling the trigger on that fateful day.

"No," she said flatly. "Because if I hadn't I would be dead. I truly believe that."

"She has a way of making everything she does look right," Hunter's aunt, Gina scoffed.

# HUSBAND KILLER : THE TRUE STORY OF MICHELLE HALL

## TORI BAKER

It's never easy being a member of a blended family. There's a certain understanding that comes along with a second or third marriage – especially one involving children – that there is going to be a fundamental need for combined effort, tolerance and compromise.

When Michelle Garner remarried for what would be the third and last time, family and friends believed she had finally found happiness after reconnecting with an old high-school flame.

John Brittson "Britt" Hall, an aircraft mechanic and home builder, had known his own fair share of heartache; he was recently divorced when he found his old high school girlfriend, Michelle, on an online dating web site.

Britt Hall and Michelle Garner first met in 1986 while attending high school in Newnan, GA. The two briefly dated before Michelle Hall graduated in 1987.

"They both were in the popular clique," forensic psychologist Robert Brion said. "Britt was a baseball player that all of the girls had a crush on. Michelle was popular herself, very outgoing with a lot of friends."

The parents of Britt and Michelle were friends as well but they didn't consider the dating relationship between Michelle and Britt to be a serious one. After graduation, Michelle would move away and she would marry a man named Rusty Hart. The couple would have two daughters until their divorce in 1996.

The single mom worked as a dental assistant to support her daughters. Times were tight until 1999 when she met and married Steve Davis.

"Steve Davis was a businessman," Brion said. "He was divorced himself with a daughter of his own. He met Michelle and quickly fell for her charms as she could come across as a very warm and caring person. He asked her to marry him after about a year of dating."

Michelle would become pregnant during the union and give birth to her third daughter, Alyssa.

Unfortunately, her second marriage met the same fate as her first and within a few years, the couple had filed for divorce, citing irreconcilable differences.

Britt did well for himself after high school, becoming an airline mechanic for Delta Airlines. He made good money with Delta until they laid him off. He then went into business with his father in home construction until ultimately returning back to Delta after they had a rehire.

His marriage started to fail, however. His first wife cited that Britt had "mental problems" and filed for divorce, stating that the marriage was "irretrievably broken."

"Britt's first wife would take him to court at least six to eight times a year after their divorce," Brion said. "He was depressed and the court visits weren't helping."

His divorce would coincide with Michelle's impending divorce with Steve Davis. Her divorce with Davis was a particularly nasty one and Britt could sympathize. They would reconnect over a dating website.

In the midst of her own divorce, Garner was happy to find love again with Britt Hall as they rekindled old flames. Shortly after reconnecting, Britt invited Michelle over for Sunday lunch with his family, and all seemed well for the couple.

"Michelle did mention to Britt's family that she was going through some difficult times with her divorce," Brion said. "She was cheerful throughout but hinted that the custody battles she was going through were quite serious."

Little did Britt Hall's family know that their excitement would soon be turned to devastation; a tragedy that would make national headlines and be detailed in various murder documentaries.

THE BRADY BUNCH

Ronald Hall, Britt's father was all to happy to have Michelle back in his son's life. At least at first.

"We visited and talked," Ronald said. "And she came in and was just as happy as she ever was," he said.

It wasn't long before Britt Hall's romance with Garner turned more serious, and the two tied the knot in September of 2006. The new marriage was an adjustment, to say the least. Britt had three children from his previous marriage and Michelle Hall had three of her own children as well. The blended family of eight was now living in Britt Hall's town home.

"You can imagine how tight the living quarters were," Brion said. "But Michelle's girls really took to their new stepfather. They became comfortable enough to call him 'Dad'."

Britt wanted a bigger home and decided to build a large home with the help of his father. The men paid for contractors to pour concrete and establish the foundation, but father and son built the majority of the house by hand.

"People didn't know where the couple were getting the money to build the house," Brion said. "But Britt did most of the work himself after the foundation was laid. So he was able to save a lot of money when it came to sweat equity. That's a testimony to how badly he wanted the marriage between he and Michelle to work out."

When all was said and done, Britt and Michelle Hall were the proud owners of a beautiful 4100 square foot home on ten acres, the perfect place to spend the rest of their lives together. The brand new house boasted vaulted ceilings, granite counter tops, and a finished basement. The construction would prove to be a house of cards, however, as things were brewing underneath the surface.

Michelle didn't have much luck with her two previous marriages, and although individual accounts may vary, her two former husbands are both to have reported being abused by Michelle during the course of their marriage.

Michelle never had a firm grasp on her emotions and didn't handle anger well. These character flaws would not bode well for her life with

Britt. Dealing with both partners' ex-spousal issues including custody and visitation, Michelle and Britt found themselves tinkering on the edge of divorce after a few months into their marriage.

"The way Britt and Michelle handled their issues were different," said family friend Sue Mathis. "Michelle was quicker to speak her mind and a lot of times, Britt just wanted her to try to gain a little bit more self-control."

Dealing with his own ex-wife and their similar divorce problems, Britt Hall was also facing his own internal battles with depression. Although he wasn't often the instigator in their frequent arguments, he was known to fervently engage in the verbal conflicts. While this certainly wasn't conducive to a happy and fruitful marriage, Britt Hall made it clear to friends he would not give up on his family and the life he had built.

The next couple of years came with continued stress, intensified by financial worries after the Halls realized they had gotten too far deep in debt as a result of building their dream home. Notices of foreclosure, liens on the house, and over-extensions were haunting the couple and causing both spouses to hit a breaking point.

On July 30, 2008, it was another typical tense day in the Hall household. Friends say Britt Hall, already aggravated due to a landscaper failing to complete a job on time, went to the store to pick-up hot dogs for a family get-together.

"Hey hon," Britt said as he called his wife. "How many hot dogs do you think I should get-"

"Count how many damn people are here," Michelle snapped. "That's how much you should get."

This would be the snide comeback that would break the straw in Britt's back. He grew tired at her constant bickering and baiting. When he came home that evening, a fight would ensue.

Michelle's youngest daughter, Alyssa, was in the living room watching television as her mother vacuumed to prepare for the company soon arriving. When Britt Hall told Alyssa to turn the TV down, another argument between the couple ensued and Hall immediately told her daughter to go upstairs to her bedroom and not come out until she was called.

There are only two individuals who know the details of what followed on that evening, and only one of them lived to tell. When all was said and done, Britt would be dead and Michelle would be charged with murder.

The 911 call came in at 8:02 p.m. by a frantic Michelle who told dispatchers that her husband had tried to kill her and commit suicide.

"He shot at me, and we were fighting to get it," Michelle told dispatchers regarding the weapon. She said she heard the gun go off twice. Seconds later, she told dispatchers her husband was turning blue.

When police arrived, Britt Hall was dead and had three noticeable gunshot wounds to his body: one on his left arm, one on his right thigh, and a close-range shot to his chest. Michelle Hall, bruised, scraped and covered in blood, told first responders the same story she had told dispatchers: her suicidal husband had tried to kill her before turning the gun on himself.

Prior to further investigation, deputies on the scene immediately called Britt Hall's parents and told them their son had committed suicide. The Halls refused to believe the news.

"Things just seemed to be going too good at this time in his life for him to have done that," said his mother, Charlene Hall. "I knew he didn't kill himself; I knew for a fact that didn't happen."

It didn't take long for police to begin seeing the crime scene a little differently than Michelle had described. Blood splatter and numerous bullet holes covered the downstairs bedroom, and a trail of blood led into the bathroom where Britt Hall's lifeless body now lay. If this was a suicide, there sure was a struggle beforehand.

Investigators gave Michelle the opportunity to explain the scene. She told how an argument between the couple turned violent when

Britt Hall threw her onto the bed. He immediately went into the study and she followed him.

Then she noticed the gun on the computer desk.

Knowing her husband was battling depression, she said she immediately became concerned with his safety, worried that he may use the gun to harm himself.

Michelle stated that she instinctively dove for the gun, and that's when Britt Hall reached for it as well and the two began struggling for possession.

After both Michelle and her husband lost control of he gun, she quickly picked up the weapon and began shooting rounds into the walls and floor in an effort to unload the gun.

In the hall, Britt Hall caught up with her and that's when she said he threatened to kill her. In yet another entanglement of an attempt for control of the gun, Michelle said the gun accidentally went off. This shot punctured Britt Hall's thigh, and that's when Hall claimed she went to call for help.

Britt Hall began crawling into the bathroom, unable to walk and calling out her name for help. When she approached him, gun in hand, she said he grabbed the pistol from her, put it to his chest, and pulled the trigger.

The problem with her story, however, was that most suicides don't entail multiple gunshot wounds. Additionally, the manner in which the fatal shot was delivered raised eyebrows for investigators.

"I've worked many suicides in my career, and I've never worked a suicide that I can remember where a man had shot himself in the chest," Lt John Lewis said.

Furthermore, the gunshot wound on Britt Hall's chest had no signs of charring or burning around the entry wound, signs which usually indicate a self-inflicted wound.

Britt Hall also had a shattered elbow and a bullet hole in his left arm. Three different shots, all which led investigators to believe they weren't being told the whole story.

Michelle did her best to persuade the investigative team to believe her story, but her story changed upon being brought to the station for questioning. While at first she claimed the two struggled for control over the gun, she then claimed Britt Hall was never actually in possession of the gun at all.

Coupled with the evidence at the crime scene and her story's inconsistencies, Michelle was charged the next morning with the murder of her husband.

Crucial to the prosecution's case was the testimony of Michelle's youngest daughter, Alyssa, who was in the home during the shooting. Police brought the 8-year-old in for questioning immediately following the incident and she clearly stated she heard her step-father pleading with her mother to "put the gun down," she said. Alyssa would ultimately testify in her mother's trial in 2009.

Facing charges of malice murder and aggravated assault, Michelle vehemently denied killing her husband. She insisted that he died of a self-inflicted gunshot wound after threatening suicide and fighting with her over the .38 caliber revolver.

The fight that evening was par for the course, she said. The two regularly got into verbal and physical altercations, and their marriage was falling apart due to financial stress. They would also constantly fight over ex-spouses, custody and visitation regarding the six children. Although there were no police reports relating to any domestic altercations in the home before, family and friends knew things weren't okay on the home front.

"Britt would spend several nights driving to work calling me and saying 'I don't know what to do.' He would have done everything in his power to save his marriage, even if it was not worth saving. He was terrified of failure," said Mathis.

One of the first fights that turned physical in front of the family was in November 2006, when Britt Hall's eldest daughter came into the room to find Michelle Hall unconscious. Her father quickly ushered her out of the room and told her not to worry about it. The next couple of years only brought more trouble due to the same old problems and Britt's alleged mental illness.

Britt was prescribed three different types of medication for depression at the time of his death, police confirmed.

But the physical evidence did not add up to suicide. Initially, the Georgia Bureau of Investigation estimated the fatal gunshot to have been fired from around 18-24 inches away. This is not consistent with suicide, detectives argued. While many victims of mental illness fall prey to suicide each year, the facts must add up. In this case, they did not.

If convicted, Michelle was facing life in prison.

In September of 2009, testimonies were heard by Alyssa Davis, as well as responding officers Capt. Tony Grant and Sgt. Freddy Cox, about what they saw and heard on the night of the shooting.

Cox testified that Hall's appearance was "consistent with someone who'd been in a physical altercation" and that Hall had bruises, scrapes and blood on her neck and forehead as well as blood on her hands and a knot on her elbow.

During his testimony, Grant stated he immediately noticed that Hall's face was red and she had what appeared to be gun-shot residue on her hand, even though she was stating her husband had committed suicide.

There were multiple bullet holes throughout the downstairs of the home when police arrived on the scene, Grant testified. Two bullets were recovered from Britt Hall's body and three more were found in the house.

Grant said a blood pattern analysis showed blood spatters of 90 degrees in the downstairs quarters outside of the bathroom, proof that Britt Hall crawled into the bathroom after being wounded.

Defense Attorney Mike Kam said that while in no uncertain terms would he call the key ear witness a liar, her age and her location during the shooting did not make for the most reliable testimony.

"She was eight; she didn't see anything, she clearly got some of the facts confused." Kam said in an interview. "She's not someone who is used to being asked questions in formal interview settings. Who knows what she remembered, or what happened?"

Additionally, Kam indicated that Michelle certainly didn't fit the description of a murderer. Outside of two divorces, Hall had no criminal record. She was law-abiding citizen, with nothing in her background which would give the assumption she was capable of murder, he said.

But the jury had heard enough. On September 25, 2009, Michelle Hall was found guilty on all counts in the death of her husband Britt.

Not long after her conviction, Hall's attorneys filed a motion for a new trial, citing trial court errors. Coweta County Superior Court Judge Jack Kirby denied the motion and the defense attorneys took the case to the Supreme Court.

On September 22, 2010, the Supreme Court of Georgia upheld the conviction, despite Hall's defense's argument that the trial court erred by admitting similar transaction evidence and prior consistent statements.

Hall's defense stated that testimony from both of her ex-husbands that she was verbally and physically abusive were inadmissible because they were not "sufficiently similar" to establish proof of the crimes for which she was charged, according to the opinion of the Supreme Court. It also stated that "in cases of domestic violence, prior incidents of abuse against family members or sexual partners are more generally permitted because there is a logical connection between violent acts against two different persons with whom the accused had a similar emotional or intimate attachment."

The opinion also added that the fifteen and thirteen-year lapses of time between her ex-husband's allegations of abuse to the alleged shooting of her husband did not require exclusion of evidence.

"Given that the similar transaction evidence reflects appellant's behavior towards prior spouses, we conclude that any prejudice from the age of these prior incidents was outweighed by the probative value of the evidence under the particular facts of this case and the purpose for which the similar transactions were offered."

Eighteen months later, however, Michelle retained a new attorney who filed a habeas corpus petition, stating Michelle was given ineffective legal counsel by Kam during her trial in 2009. Senior Judge Robert B. Struble presided over the hearing and determined that Hall was in-fact entitled to a new trial. Struble agreed that Kam, Hall's trial attorney, was "ineffective and fell below the minimum guarantee of representation under the constitution," a press release said.

While Michelle may have been looking forward to another chance at redemption, The Attorney General's Office quickly announced their plans to appeal the habeas corpus ruling to the Georgia Supreme Court.

In a press release on March 30, 2012, Coweta County District Attorney Peter John Skandalakis expressed his respectful disapproval of the court's ruling and that in stating Kam was ineffective for representation, "the court erroneously applied the wrong standard under the law."

Skandalakis said he was optimistic that the Supreme Court will conclude that Hall had a legally sufficient defense and that her conviction would be upheld after review of the appeal.

On January 22, 2013, the Supreme Court found Hall's convictions to be fair and just, denying insufficient representation during her 2009 trial. According to the court summary, the Supreme Court concluded that the habeas corpus petition did not conduct proper legal analysis to determine the effectiveness of Hall's defense.

The opinion references Strickland v. Washington, a 1984 Supreme Court case in which it determined that to be granted a new trial, a defendant must show that it was due to insufficient performance by defense that the defendant was found guilty.

Michelle's argument for her habeas corpus petition was that "if she were in the same room when her young daughter was questioned, she could have assisted her attorney by prompting him with specific information," the court says in its opinion. However, it was determined during the habeas hearing that any information she would have portrayed to her attorney was already known information to both parties. "As such, Hall has failed to show actual prejudice, and her claim of ineffective assistance of counsel should have been rejected," the opinion said.

Today, Michelle Hall remains in a Coweta County prison.

Since her conviction, Michelle's ex-husbands have been given full custody of her three respective daughters.

She won't be eligible for parole until 2039. She will be 70 years old.

# HUSBAND KILLER MICHELLE REYNOLDS

## GARY GUIDEN

On July 5th, 2004, a Frito Lay delivery pulled into the empty parking lot of a distribution center in Rome, Georgia. The man noticed that another man- one he didn't recognize- was coming out of the office, and although someone in the office in the early morning hours wasn't unusual, not recognizing the man was. According to the diver, the man who came into view appeared to be nervous- looking over his shoulder, glancing around, and checking behind him.

The man, possibly unaware of the delivery driver still sitting in his vehicle, exits the building and enters a mini-van after removing his shirt. Thinking this was odd, the delivery driver entered the Frito Lay office only to discover the scene of a horror film.

He discovered the slumped over body of the regional manager, Thad Reynolds, sitting in a pool of his own blood. He called 911 and EMT's and police officers responded within minutes. However, it was too late. Thad Reynolds was dead before anyone arrived.

Ross Cavitt, a reporter at the scene, noted that Reynolds had been stabbed 19 times. Due to the nature of the stab wounds and the amount of blood, it was obvious to Cavitt that there had been a great struggle.

Thad's death sent shock through his community, but hit his church, the Hollywood Baptist, the hardest as Thad and his wife Michelle were well-known within the church community. In her early days, Michelle had been popular in high school and well respected within her community.

Thad, on the other hand, was a dedicated Christian and devoted father to his 4 children, as well as a loving husband to his wife, Michelle. As a young man, Thad had been heavily involved in sports and was popular at his high school.

"He could always make your day better" stated Julie Crumbley about her late friend Thad.

Michelle was a mother of 4 and a likeable person, according to Thad's close friend, Julie Crumbley.

Before becoming a mother, Michelle had worked as an administrative assistant, but had given the job up after giving birth to her first child in 1992. After the couple began to have children, the decision was made that Michelle would be a stay at home mom and raise their children.

In 1995, however, the couple's relationship took a turn for the worse and Michelle asked for a divorce. Thad's sister, Beverly Owners, claims that Michelle hadn't been happy just being a mother and a wife. It's been said that Michelle had made the following comment to a pastor at the couple's church: "You put your wife on a pedestal, but Thad never put me on a pedestal."

Thad agreed to the divorce, but regretted his decision as he didn't believe in divorce or broken homes. Undone by the divorce, Thad turned to his church for help. Two years after their divorce, the couple remarried, built a new home, and added more children to their family.

Thad's career began to flourish, after he was hired into the Frito Lay company where he was able to work his way to district manager. He also sang in the church's choir and served as a deacon, as well as helped other couples with marriage counseling.

"They appeared to be the most perfect family whenever you would see them" says Crumbley.

Thad's mother told Dateline that the couple had been called Barbie and Ken because of how well their life seemed to be going.

Both Michelle and Thad had a passion for children and worked with the church's youth group to put on shows, skits, and performances in various locations. They worked closely with the church's youth minister, Scott Harper and his wife, Paige. Thad and Scott became best friends and the families became joined at the hip. Paige and Michelle also became close, bonding over their stay at home lifestyles and busy husbands.

So, what went wrong? The answer to this was revealed only after a shocking truth involving Michelle and her best friend's husband came to light.

In 2004, Thad decided to become a minister, as he felt that God was calling to him to join the ministry. In June of that year, Michelle signed up to help the Harper family with a youth retreat, but called Paige shortly before they were set to leave and said that she had had a change of heart.

"She called me last minute and said that she was going to book her own room and was not going to room with me, because she needed her own time" says Paige, when asked about the phone call. This meant that Michelle would be the only chaperon who had her own private room.

"Michelle was distant. She wouldn't speak to me or look me in the eye" Paige says. Paige grew concerned and confronted her best friend. "I said "Michelle is there something wrong? Have I done something to offend you?" and she looked me in the eye and said no, I just want to be around people who are on fire for God."

As her husband prepared to become a minister, Michelle began to spend less time with Paige and more time with her husband, Scott.

"She would constantly be asking him for assistance. More and more she would ask him for help working with the children or how to do certain things with them. They began to email and communicate" says prosecutor, Leigh Patterson.

On Saturday, July 3rd, 2004, the Harper and Reynolds' met up for a long weekend celebration. The next day, a Sunday, the met up once again to attend church together. That day, the families met at a local park to play volleyball, gave snacks, and enjoy each other's company.

"I noticed Michelle being kind of flirtatious towards other men, asking somebody to help her throw a football and stuff like that." Paige says.

"She was a little bit too flirty...wanting other men to pay attention to her" agrees Patterson.

Despite Michelle's odd behavior at the picnic, she and her husband loaded up their children at the end of the evening and went home like nothing had happened.

The next morning Thad left for work before sunrise and while Michelle and the kids were still asleep. After only a few minutes at the office, a van pulled up outside of the office where Thad was working. The driver was Scott Harper, and within a few minutes, Thad would be dead on the floor of his office.

On July 5th, when Thad's body was discovered, the city of Rome, Georgia was thrown into chaos.

The first question on investigator's lips was who would launch a violent attack on the well-loved church deacon?

"There were wounds all over his body, including defensive wounds" says Patterson.

The only witness had been the delivery driver who had discovered Thad's body, but he had been unable to get a good look at Thad's attacker's face or the license plate of the van he had been driving.

Upon investigation of the scene, it became apparent to police that Thad had managed to wound his attacker. This was proved by a large amount of blood that was found by the office doorway- blood that matched up with the delivery driver's statement claiming that the unknown man stopped by the door before getting into his van and leaving the scene.

Also on the scene, police found the empty case for a hunting knife and a pair of glasses. The glasses also matched up with witness testimony, as the man was seen removing his shirt and in doing so, his glasses could have fallen off and been left behind in his haste to get away.

Scott Harper was called to help identify Thad's body and was one of the first people to learn of his death. Scott called his wife and upon hearing the news, Paige become worried about Michelle.

The Harpers drove to the Reynolds house to be with Michelle, however, upon arrival, they found that the church's head pastor was already there.

According to family and friends, Michelle has taken the news stoically.

"You would think that when we got there, Michelle would come and give us a hug or cry and she didn't" said Beverly Owens, surprised at how Michelle took the news.

Thad's mother also noticed Michelle's lack of outward emotion and was concerned by it.

"She had just bought a black dress about two weeks before and made the comment "whoever thought that I'd be using it for this.""

Meanwhile, back at the crime scene, investigators had begun to wonder about Thad's death. To them, it didn't appear to be a random attack and robbery situation, but seemed to have been calculated and planned, as Thad's murderer didn't take any of his money or anything that he had had on him. The reason behind the attack appeared to be one thing: to kill Thad Reynolds.

On the news that evening, a clue was unearthed as to who could have killed the deacon. Scott Roberts, a coworker of Scott Harper, had heard the news asking for leads and picked up the phone almost immediately.

Roberts called the police department and reported to the officials that his coworker, Scott Harper was both friends with Thad and drove a burgundy minivan like the one that had been witnessed leaving the crime scene.

Roberts was asked for a statement and while telling them what he knew, he alerted the police that Scott Harper had been having an affair with someone- information that he claimed he had stumbled upon without meaning to. Roberts worked with phonelines and was tasked with fixing them. A few weeks before the murder, he had tapped into a conversation to fix the phoneline and overheard Harper talking to a woman who wasn't his wife, Paige. He had also overheard that the woman's name was Michelle.

"They were flirting. Lover chit chat, if you will. Kind of reminded me of high school sweethearts" said Roberts in an interview with Dateline.

Officials ended their interview with Roberts by asking a simple question- did Harper wear glasses? Roberts had answered that, yes, Scott Harper did wear glasses.

This left police to wonder were the connections between the van, the glasses, and a possible affair all just coincidence? Or was there something sinister going on?

The Harpers were then brought in for official questioning, where Scott told investigators that he had hurt his hand at the gym, when he was asked why his hand was bandaged. This explained his hand but didn't explain why his glasses were missing.

Scott was released, despite police not believing his story. Paige was starting to doubt her husband, as well.

"When we left the station, I asked him if he knew anything about Thad's murder...about what was going on" Paige said "and he said "do you realize what you're asking me?""

Police obtained a warrant to search Scott's computer at the hospital that he worked at, in hopes of getting answers. They had a particular interest to look into Scott's emails, as they were saved on a public server and could be easily accessed.

It was found that a large portion of the emails were to and from Thad's wife, Michelle. At first, the emails were innocent- mostly consisting of routine topics such as the youth group that Michelle worked with at the church. Gradually, though, the emails became more personal and revealing in nature.

About a month before the death of her husband, the tone of the emails changed.

"She was coming onto him in the emails. Usually under the guise of I know I shouldn't feel this way" Patterson says, referring to Michelle and the emails that she sent to Scott "and he fell for it."

"The emails, especially toward the end, were very graphic and specific" said prosecutor Natalee Staats.

It wasn't clear from the emails when their affair became physical, however, records show that at the youth retreat in June, Scott had booked Michelle's room and stayed in it with her. Paige, although quiet about the whole thing, had noticed Scott get up and leave the room and noted that he didn't return until the next morning.

"He had gone down to Michelle's room and even though they were on a church trip with kids and his wife, and Michelle's daughter there as a participant, they had continued their affair" said Patterson.

Police combed over every detail of their emails, but couldn't decide whether Michelle had coaxed Scott into murdering her husband or not. According to Patterson, Michelle had been very careful with what she said and how she said it.

"Michelle never said "I need you to kill my husband" said Staats. However, she hinted at the idea by sayings things like "You'll have to live longer than Thad for us to be together because he'll never agree to divorce."

After Michelle had planted the idea in Scott's head, he had gone on to lookup poison and arsenic, as well an essay on how to commit the perfect murder Patterson reported.

On the evening of July 4th, hours before the murder would happen, the two exchanged a final round of emails.

"The night before, she tells him what Thad's schedule was going to be the next morning. Specific directions of where he was going to be" she also reports.

"Those were all glaring clues to the police that Michelle might have been involved in a conspiracy to murder her husband" said Staats, in agreeance with Patterson.

Scott had sent Michelle an email giving her an out. The email told Michelle to tell him if she had any hesitations, and that if she did, he wouldn't go through with it. Michelle replied that didn't have any hesitations and was ready for the event to take place.

Scott Harper was charged with murder on July 8th, 2004 after he turned himself in. He was charged with murder, felony murder, aggravated assault, and aggravated battery.

Authorities hoped that Scott would tie Michelle into the case, however, Scott was blinded by his feelings for her and was willing to protect her at all costs. He invoked the right to remain silent and didn't make another statement for or against Michelle's innocence.

Michelle was also arrested, as police had enough evidence from Michelle's own emails, that she had been involved.

"Once they figured it out, they decided pretty quickly that they had enough to charge her as well" said Michelle's attorney, Jim Berry.

An hour or so after Scott had turned himself in, Michelle was placed under arrest and brought into police custody and like her lover, Michelle refused to talk.

"Michelle was arrested as she came out of her attorney's office in downtown Rome" said Patterson.

"I had no clue. Everybody seemed happy" said Paige, who was shocked by the news that Michelle and Scott were in custody.

"Friends that they interacted with at the church didn't dream that the family pastor was having an affair with the deacon's wife" Patterson said.

The fact that Michelle and Scott could and would conspire to murder Thad Reynolds was unthinkable to the members of the church, who knew both people as being kind and good-hearted.

Scott Roberts, after hearing the news, took it upon himself to search the hospital where he and Scott worked for anything that police might have missed. He focused on the IT department's data center and more specifically, he focused on the tile floor. He was able to lift up a tile using a suction cup, and underneath, found the item that would be pinned as the murder weapon: a hunting knife. He also discovered a pile of bloody clothes.

In November, 4 months after Thad's murder, Michelle and Scott were summoned to the court room for a preliminary hearing to decide who would be tried first.

"The state gets to elect, by law, who to try first. We had elected to try her first" said Patterson. The decision to try Michelle first was a risk, as her case was the weaker of the two. Prosecutors knew that she hadn't bene the one to physically take Thad's life, however, they held her responsible for the murder.

"She was the person that made it happen" said Ross Cavitt "even though Scott Harper had the murder weapon in his hand, they could see that he was following orders from Michelle which made her ultimately responsible for the crime."

The emails, although suspicious, didn't pin Michelle to giving the orders, but prosecutors hoped that Harper would. They hoped that by presenting him with the evidence that was quickly stacking against him, they would be able to convince him to cut a deal and turn his back on Michelle.

Aside from the leverage of evidence that prosecutors had, the DA had written and notified the court that she would be seeking the death penalty for both Scott and Michelle.

"After the death of a fine young man, a father of four, to seek the death penalty wasn't that surprising" said Cavitt, in regard to the DA's email.

All that was left for prosecutors to do was wait and hope that Scott would cave.

"I had begged Scotty to do what was needed and to give up the information, and to tell the story of his involvement and Michelle's involvement" Paige told Dateline "and he would always tell me no, to just leave her out of this"

"He was smitten and head over heels in love with her" Cavitt said.

"I think that she couldn't have cared less about him. I think he was just the muscle behind the act" said Patterson, who was convinced that Michelle had simply used Harper's infatuation with her to get him to do her bidding.

Despite the prosecutor's hopes, Harper continued to clam up when it came to Michelle's involvement. It seemed that even the threat of the death penalty wasn't enough to get him to talk.

Years passed this way.

"Meetings with him resulted in nothing. He would not come forward" said Staats.

Finally, in the fall of 2008 and 4 years after both parties had been locked behind bars, Scott was ready to cooperate with prosecutors.

Scott's attorneys helped him decide on a deal and upon this conversation, it became to clear to everyone involved that Harper was still infatuated with Michelle as his concern for her took center stage. He would take a life sentence and plead guilty, as long as the death penalty was taken off of Michelle's case. He did, however, agree to testify at Michelle's trial.

"He effectively saved and betrayed her at the same time" said one of his attorneys.

In the court room on October 1st, 2008, Harper sat with prosecutors and told them his account of Thad's death.

"He told us that he still loved her and he was going to do anything in his power to minimize her involvement" said Patterson

"Michelle had basically said that Thad would not leave easily. He would fight for her and not give up on their marriage and that it would get ugly" said another of his attorneys "and he said that he could deal with ugly."

After this conversation, according to Scott, he had purchased the hunting knife and the next day, he had had lunch with Michelle. The two had parked and kissed in the back seat like a pair of teenagers, and it was during this time that Michelle had asked him if he had talked to her husband yet. When he told her that he hadn't, Michelle withdrew her affection and became cold and distant towards him.

Scott said that he had been afraid of losing her, so four days later he had woken up before dawn and driven to the Frito Lay distribution center with the intent to deal with Thad Reynolds.

As he entered the building, Thad had looked up and asked him what he was doing there. Scott Harper had replied with "I want what you got."

Harper's story was not enough to pin the murder on Michelle: it was only enough to charge her with adultery.

"All it would take was for one person on the jury to say that okay. Maybe Michelle really did think that Scott was just going to talk to her husband" Patterson said.

On January 13th, 2010, Michelle was brought back into court after 6 years of being in jail. The officials and attorneys present had been expecting for Harper to testify against Michelle, however, this did not happen. Michelle stood before the jury and plead guilty to voluntary manslaughter.

"Getting Scott Harper's statement was like pulling teeth and she didn't think we'd get it. That's the only reason that she plead guilty"

" She knew that she was responsible for the death, in some way, because of the affair and because of that she felt that she should plead guilty to something" said Scott's attorney.

At the hearing that day, Thad's mother asked Michelle why her son had had to die for this.

"There was no response" said Thad's mother, Kittie Walker, "her eyes were just cold. No remorse, no feelings, nothing."

"She knew that Thad would not have let her take the kids away" said Beverly Owens "and she knew that that was the only way to get him out of the picture"

In the end, she was sentenced to 20 years behind bars, with credit being given to the time she had already served in county jail. Until her release, Michelle is unable to see her children and will lose custody of them.

According to Scott Roberts, there were people who upon hearing her sentencing, didn't feel as if justice had been served.

"I would have liked to see Michelle get a lot more time for it. I would have liked to see her life in prison" said Kittie Walker.

Many people in Rome, Georgia agreed that although Scott had wielded the knife, Michelle was the villain behind the plot.

"We're in a religious town and I think that many people believed that Scotty had been manipulated by her and that she was the devil incarnate" said Jim Berry.

Despite the tension and hard feelings, Paige Harper was visibly shaken by the case.

"Scott and Michelle were the two most important people in my life other than my kids, so for this to happen…it really makes me wonder how well I know people" she said.

In the aftermath of the murder, Thad's mother got custody of the kids and Paige divorced her husband in 2005. Despite writing letters in the early days of their sentences, Michelle and Scott have stopped communicating.

Within recent years, Michelle has written to officials asking why she isn't allowed to see her children.

"We do it all the time with adults- no contact with whomever. That's not anything new. That's a standard law order in nearly every murder case I've had, even if they're in the same family" responded Patterson, who also stated that Michelle is well aware of this order as it was part of her plea deal back in January of 2010.

Judge J. Bryant Durham, who had found Michelle guilty in years prior, mentioned that once her children turn 18 they can visit her in prison. Currently, this means that Michelle's eldest daughter, 22-year old Alisan and her infant grandchild can visit her in prison whenever they wish.

"Like it or not, if she decides to go over there every day, I don't think that can be stopped" Durham told Patterson.

The intent of the order was to restrict visitation until Michelle was released, however, due to lack of specifics and bad wording, the age of visitation remains 18.

There's no question that a good man died for less than good reasons, but there are still questions in the minds of his family and friends. Why had it happened? Had death really been Michelle's only option? It's up for speculation and, unfortunately, no one will ever know for sure.